WISE FOOLS IN SHAKESPEARE

WISE FOOLS IN SHAKESPEARE

BY ROBERT HILLIS GOLDSMITH

With an Introduction by
OSCAR JAMES CAMPBELL

MICHIGAN STATE UNIVERSITY PRESS
1963

Library of Congress Catalog Card Number: 55-11686

East Lansing, Michigan

Third Printing

PRINTED IN THE UNITED STATES OF AMERICA

TO MARY

PREFACE

THIS IS A CRITICAL STUDY of the wise fool in the plays of Shakespeare and his contemporaries. But to render Shakespeare's wise fool thoroughly intelligible to the reader, I have reviewed briefly the popular and literary traditions. The figure in the eared hood and motley coat, because of some real or assumed defect of mind, was maintained by a person of rank for amusement. His characteristic behavior, as entertainer, licensed critic, and ironical observer of folly, derived from various sources. He had the gayety of the jongleur, the candor of the ancient poets and philosophers, and the ironical perception of a Socrates. He sometimes combined a shrewd, proverbial wit with the more than earthly wisdom of the Erasmian fool.

Shakespeare uses the tradition of the fool but transcends it. He gives us not merely a theatrical type but four complex and individual characters. Each of the four—Touchstone, Lavache, Feste, and Lear's Fool—is clearly differentiated from the others. I have tried to show that Touchstone is a comic realist astray in the forest of romance, that Feste is an artist who observes the golden mean in loving and laughing, and that Lear's Fool embodies the Christian doctrine of wise folly on abandoning his prudence to follow his sick King. Since the fool often comments satirically on his fellows, I have sought to show that he differs markedly, both in the matter and the manner of his satire, from those other commentators—the malcontent and the railing buffoon. Touchstone, travestying the pastoral lovers and bantering the wise-seeming Jaques, epitomizes the fool as a genial humorist. I acknowledge my indebtedness to those scholars and editors whose writings have helped to shape my opinions. I thank the directors and librarians of the Folger Shakespeare Library for their assistance in making available to me their rich store of sixteenth-century literature. When I have cited later standard editions of plays such as Kittredge's edition of *Shakespeare's Complete Works*, I have done so because these are more readily accessible. Above all, I express my gratitude to Professors Alfred B. Harbage and Oscar J. Campbell for their care and patience in reading the manuscript. My deepest debt of gratitude I owe my wife, without whose encouragement this book would never have been written.

Emory and Henry College R. H. G.
June, 1955

INTRODUCTION

Dr. Goldsmith has designed his excellent volume for everyone concerned with Shakespeare—scholars, teachers, actors, readers and spectators. But it is audiences that should profit most from this study. For they are almost always bored and confused by the antics of the Fool on the stage, even of such popular figures as Touchstone of AS YOU LIKE IT or Feste of TWELFTH NIGHT. The Fool's costume often strikes modern spectators as silly and his grotesque properties as puzzling, if not repellent. His motley costume, in modern productions usually a thing of shreds and patches, his bauble, a parody of a King's scepter, surmounted by a fantastically carved head with asses' ears seem like elaborate absurdity. Moreover his verbal buffooneries, his play on words, his parody of the syllogism sound like gibberish.

The modern actor who takes the part is likely to alienate the spectator still further by skipping and leaping aimlessly about the stage, by shaking his bauble and singing snatches of song in an ill-trained voice.

This reaction of a modern audience to the droll business of the Fool is unfortunate. For to miss the significance of this strange figure is to lose some of the most striking dramatic effects that Shakespeare and his fellows expected the wise Fool to make. One need only call to mind the emotion-packed scenes between Lear and his Fool to realize how crucial his functions could be.

Dr. Goldsmith, with a nice sense of theatric values, examines the contribution made by the wise Fool to the unique character of a few of Shakespeare's most popular dramas. The author deals only briefly with the origin and historical development of this fellow in an eared hood and motley jacket. In the interest of clarity, however, he has thought it necessary to differentiate him from the witty jesting servant like Speed in THE TWO GENTLEMEN OF VERONA and the stupid loutlike Launce in the same play. But most of his comments are critical and aesthetic.

Since the Court Fool in real life could be free to the point of impudence with his comments upon even his master's conduct without inviting punishment, his representative in a play could naturally serve as the author's mouthpiece. The name of Touchstone suggests that this Fool's facetious wisdom was a criterion by which the actions of the other characters in AS YOU LIKE IT were judged. In his eyes even Rosalind and Orlando were betrayed by their love into folly. Yet his speech in harmony with his grotesque costume purges his ridicule of any trace of venom or harshness. What he says is always an invitation to merriment, to laughter that in retrospect becomes thoughtful. He was thus a far-off ancestor of the *raisonneur* of modern French drama and its imitators. He usually voices some form of common sense. Sometimes it takes the form of a satire, sometimes of parody, and with Lear's faithful Fool it is a quaint reminder of his master's folly, remembrance of which the old King has resolutely sought to keep suppressed.

Everyone who delights in Shakespeare in the library as well as in the theatre should find Dr. Goldsmith's volume a very present aid to the understanding and the enjoyment of Shakespeare. If actors cast in the role would read the book, they might learn how to present the figure more nearly as Shakespeare conceived it. When that happy day arrives, no one need continue to regard the Fool and his business with aversion or mere tolerance. An audience then will be as receptive to the Fool's teasing, full of mirth and flashes of insight as were those of Elizabethans lucky enough to be in the theatre when the dramas were first produced.

Oscar James Campbell

Columbia University
New York
June 28, 1955

CONTENTS

Chapter I. THE FOOL OF TRADITION

WHEN JACQUES FIRST MEETS the fool in the forest, he instantly recognizes Touchstone as a court fool by his garb. "Motley's the only wear!" (*A.Y.L.* II, vii, 34) he remarks and goes on to consider the privileges belonging to the fool's profession. Lear's Fool enters the play proffering his coxcomb to Kent (*Lear* I, iv, 105). And Lavache speaks of his bauble, the emblem of the fool's office (*All's W.* IV, v, 32). So we piece together out of these scattered allusions in the plays the patched garments of the motley fool.

Although Shakespeare nowhere explicitly states the fact, the court or domestic fool usually was bald or he wore his hair shorn like a monk's. Dondolo, in Marston's *Parasitaster: or The Fawne* (1604–1606), is specifically described as "A bald foole" in the list of characters at the beginning of the play. He is also twitted on his baldness by Herod: "thy head is alwaies working, it roles, and it roles *Dondolo*, but it gathers no mosse *Dondolo*" (I, ii, 36).[1] That the practice of shaving the fool's head was customary may be readily seen. A character in a fifteenth century French mystery play mocks Saint Peter in the following words:

> Look at that apostle!
> He is shorn like a fool.[2]

Francis Douce suggests, in his dissertation *On the Clowns and Fools of Shakspeare*, that the fool frequently shaved the head "in imitation or perhaps ridicule of a monk's crown."[3] The only trouble with Douce's inference is that the fool's custom probably antedates the monk's by several centuries. In his discourse on human vanity, Cornelius Agrippa describes certain hypocrite monks:

> . . . with shauen heades as ideotes, in theire hoodes
> made with eares & beset with belles much like to fooles.[4]

Looking further back, we read in Lucian of a jester with his head closely shaved except for a tuft left at the top in the shape of a cock's comb.[5] The mimic fool of the *phlyakes* farces of Southern Italy in the third century B.C. is represented on terra cotta vases as bald-headed or wearing a conical shaped hat or *pilos*.[6] Geoffrey of Monmouth provides us with a possible link between the ancient mime and the medieval fool in his fictional history of the old British kings. A certain Saxon warrior named Baldulf craftily disguises himself in the following manner in order to pass through the enemy's lines: "he shaved off his hair and his beard, and did upon him the habit of a jongleur with a ghittern."[7]

The fool resembled the monk not only in the cut of his hair but in the cut of his hood as well. The chief difference, as Erasmus' Pandocheus slyly points out, is in the addition of ears and bells to the fool's hood.[8] The long, drooping ears, a constant feature in the costume of all court fools, were obviously asses' ears conventionalized. Barclay welcomes the wrathful man aboard his ship of fools and assigns him this badge of his office:

> Assys erys for our folys a lyuray is
> And he that wyll be wroth for a thynge of nought
> Of the same leuray is nat worthy to mys . . .[9]

But startling proof of the long life of this particular tradition comes to us in a terra cotta figure of a Roman mime wearing a close-fitting eared hood much resembling that worn by the later court fool.[10]

In some of Douce's illustrations (plates ii, iv), the central crest of the fool's cap rises and is developed into the head and neck of a cock; in others, only a cock's comb appears. Some fools wear a single feather in addition to the cock's comb. Dieterich, with more zeal than logic, tries to trace the cock as a type of the vain, foolish warrior from *Cicirrus* of the Atellane farce down to Mr. Punch of the puppet shows.[11] But it is difficult to see how the court fool, though he does wear the crest of a cock, can be fitted into that tradition. Occasionally, the fool may have worn a fox tail hanging from behind. At least Godfrey Gobylyve, in Stephen Hawes' poem, seems to have worn such an appendage to his fool's habit:

> To vs came rydynge on a lytell nagge
> A folysshe dwarfe nothynge for the warre
> With a hood/ a bell/ a foxtayle/ and a begge
> In a pyed cote he rode brygge a bragge.[12]

But the Vice in *King Darius* (1565) probably carries the tail attached to a bladder, as the fool of the festival play does.

> Iniquytie. He dyd here so on me rayle.
> But I thynke, I gaue hym a blowe
> with a foxe tayle.[13]

The wearing of a fox tail brings to mind the fool or "Captain Cauf Tail" of the ploughboy plays and village morris dances.

The asses' ears, the coxcomb, and the occasional fox tail combine to suggest that the fool derived his dress from some sort of primitive animal masquerade. Chambers sees these items of the fool's clothing as conventionalized survivals of the old sacrificial *exuviae*.[14] But the actors in the early fertility rites were deeply in earnest and wore their grotesque costumes not to amuse an idle audience but to placate the harsh gods of the wind and the weather. Pickard-Cambridge has a theory that Attic comedy originated from animal masquerades and processions, but he attaches no special religious significance to these spectacles. Instead, he believes that the comic spirit springs from man's childlike delight in whimsey and playful mimicry.[15] If he is right, then some articles in the fool's wardrobe may well go back to the very dawn of comedy.

Most court fools wore a long coat or jerkin of motley usually. On state occasions, the fool's habit may have been more elaborate, exhibiting the parti-colored pattern minutely described in a semi-official record of 1605, quoted by Petit de Julleville:

> . . . [The suit] is made from strips of serge, half green and half yellow; and where there are yellow strips, there is green trimming; between the strips there is also yellow and green taffeta, which is stitched to the said strips and trimming. The hose is sewed to the breeches, one [leg] all of green serge and the other of yellow, and the cap also, half yellow half green, with ears.[16]

Fool's garments were sometimes made of costly fabrics, as this description suggests. Bilioso, in Marston's *The Malcontent* (1604), proposes to dress his Passarello in velvet to distinguish him from the common run of fools who wear only satin (III, i, 63). As for the colors, green and yellow seem to have predominated, although red was occasionally added. Samuel Rowley's Will Summers must have worn "a long motley coat guarded [trimmed] with yellow" if we may judge from the Prologue to Shakespeare and Fletcher's *King Henry the Eighth*.[17] Natural fools and idiots often wore long, yellow gowns, simply for decency's sake. But such a cassock would be ill-suited to the court fool who was also a tumbler and a dancer.

Flögel attempts to show that the bells which studded the fool's costume came jingling down to him from the official robes of the Jewish High Priest of antiquity.[18] This explanation for the fool's bells seems rather farfetched and unnecessary when we recall that medieval knights and demoiselles went about the banquet hall and the tourney-yard with bells on their bracelets and bells on their toes. In mimicking this court folly, the fool merely wore more bells and kept up the fad longer. That the wearing of bells may still have been *de rigeur* in the mid-thirteenth century is suggested by Ralph Simnell's merry quip in Greene's play.

RAPHE. And, sirha Lacie, buy me a thousand thousand million of fine bels.
LACIE. What wilt thou do with them, Raphe?
RAPHE. Mary, every time that Ned sighs for the keepers daughter, Ile tie a bell about him: and so within three or foure daies I will send word to his father Harry, that his sonne, and my maister Ned, is become Loves morris dance.[19]

In discussing the fool's accoutrements, we come now to his marotte or bauble. This ranged from a rough stick with an attached bladder to a finely wrought scepter tipped with a fool's head in miniature. The obvious inference is that the fool reigned over his followers with a bauble as the king ruled with his scepter or the Lord Mayor with his mace. However, there is another, more primitive explanation for the bauble that the fool carried. Douce observes that the form of the fool's bauble was sometimes "obscene in the highest degree."[20] There is surely a double entendre in two references to a bauble in Shakespeare's plays. Mercutio uses a bawdy simile to describe Romeo's infatuation for Rosaline: "this drivelling love is like a great natural that runs lolling up and down to hide his bauble in a hole" (II, iv, 95). Lavache jokes in much the same tenor with Lafeu:

LAFEU. Whether dost thou profess thyself—a knave or a fool?
CLOWN. A fool, sir, at a woman's service, and a knave at a man's.
LAF. Your distinction?
CLOWN. I would cozen the man of his wife and do his service.
LAF. So you were a knave at his service indeed.
CLOWN. And I would give his wife my bauble, sir, to do her service. (*All's W.* IV, v, 23)

Is it not conceivable that the medieval fool's bauble was but a vestige of the exaggerated phallus worn by the Dorian mime and the mimic fool of the later *phlyakes*? In the processions of the *phallophoroi*, it should be noted, the participants carried the symbol of male fertility mounted upon a pole.[21] If an association can be established between the fool's bauble and the phallus of the bald-headed mime, we should have one more proof of the ancient origin of the court fool's costume.

It would be the height of folly, however, to try to reconstruct the fool and his history merely from an examination of his characteristic clothing. First of all, the domestic and court fool did not always wear the official motley (Douce, II, 325). And in the second place, some of those who formerly wore the eared hood, the coxcomb, or the motley dress had little else in common with the professional jester. The bald-headed fool began his theatrical career as a travesty upon the mythological Herakles and Odysseus and ended as the *stupidus* of the early Roman Empire.[22] The circus clown of today, who stumbles as he tries to imitate the acrobats, is in the direct line of descent from this Roman mime. The *Cicirrus*, who may have worn a coxcomb as a part of his comic mask, belongs in the tradition of the plumed Greek *alazon* and the Roman *miles gloriosus;* types more foolish than fooling. In the comedies of the renaissance, the swaggering captain was often the butt of the clever *zanni*, *badin*, or witty fool. And *Arlecchino* of the *Commedia dell'Arte*, although he too wore a patched or parti-colored suit, exhibited a very different kind of humor from that of the motley fool. Not so much witty in himself as a cause for wit in others, *Arlecchino* resembled the antique buffoon and the whimsical sot.[23] None of these figures, however, shows much similarity to the court fool. All have but one trait in common—the ability to evoke laughter.

As an entertainer pure and simple—and he was that before all else—the professional fool was probably related to the medieval minstrel and *joculator*, who roamed Europe after the breakup of the Empire and the collapse of the Roman stage. Like the minstrel, he was often a ballad singer, dancer, and tumbler. And like the *joculator*, whom he more closely resembled, he was frequently a fleering and obscene jester or parodist.[24] As Douce (II, 307) reminds us, the buffoon and minstrel were often united in the same person in early times. Shakespeare's Feste combines in himself the witty fool and the gay minstrel. In his repertory he includes the songs of the *trouvère* and the tavern singer, for as he asks Sir Toby and Sir Andrew: "Would you have a love song, or a song of good life?" (*Twel.* II, iii, 36). The names *jongleur (jugler, joglar)*, *joculator*, and *gestator* (*gestour*, jester) seem never to have been clearly and consistently differentiated, and the types they represented were constantly merging one into the other.[25] At some time in the early middle ages, the traveling entertainer—jester, juggler, or minstrel—began to look for a home with some prince or great lord. Meanwhile a place was preparing for him in the privileged role of the household fool.

The custom of keeping natural fools or dwarfs may be traced back to Roman times, when people sometimes kept monstrous imbeciles as pets much as ladies of a later day kept monkeys (Flögel, p. 159). These mental defectives were bought at public auction in the monster-market, and the more foolish they were, the better was the price that they brought.[26] The practice of maintaining fools for the sake of the amusement they afforded grew during the medieval period, and kings, nobles, and some princes of the church assumed the guardianship of these deformed and defective creatures. To a modern, it seems crude and even cruel to laugh at the rambling wits of a moron. But it must be remembered that even so fine and humane a person as Sir Thomas More kept his domestic fool, Patteson.

Before we too hastily censure our ancestors for their callous sense of humor, we ought to remember that they lived before the days of clinical psychology. Insane persons were flogged in darkened cells in order to drive out the demons that obviously had possession of their minds. Even the well-meaning half-wit sometimes felt the bite of the whip when it was administered for the good of his immortal soul. Also far back in the racial memory of man was the taboo that set apart the divine madman or the fool as a kind of seer. The popular mind even in Shakespeare's day looked on these "innocents," as they were called, with mingled feelings of awe, amused contempt, and something like pity. Out of this mixed attitude toward the fool grew his license to speak freely and behave capriciously.

We should remember in passing that the "all-licensed fool" of tradition never had the complete immunity from punishment that he is sometimes thought to have enjoyed.[27] Though Olivia finds "no slander in an allow'd fool" (*Twel.* I, v, 101), her servingwoman Maria jests mordantly with Feste, "My lady will hang thee for thy absence" (I, v, 3). Should he not take this threat too seriously, Maria dangles over Feste's head the danger of being turned away from Olivia's household to become a "vagabond or sturdy beggar" on the highways of late Elizabethan England. Numerous statutes had been published throughout the Tudor period providing for the apprehension and punishment of all such masterless men.[28] Touchstone, Will Summers, and Lear's Fool live constantly under the threat of the whip. We may assume that when Will Summers went to sleep with the spaniels it was on no bed of roses. Nevertheless, the natural fool or idiot was tolerated and was allowed a measure of freedom not permitted the other lower domestics. The freedom to indulge in wanton talk, truth-telling, and parody proved an incentive strong enough to enlist many perfectly sane men in the ranks of counterfeit fools.[29]

Since the man in motley enjoyed this privileged, if somewhat eccentric, position in the medieval court or manor house, what was more natural than that the itinerant jester or *joculator* should disguise his wits and assume the role of domestic fool? Part of the *joculator's* reason for being disappeared as the printing of books increased and the demand for oral story-tellers declined. The office of fool, degraded as it sometimes was, yet offered a haven of security and an escape from obloquy. In exchange for this security and the right to practice his profession, the *joculator* was ready enough to pull-on the coxcomb and bells over his already shaved head. Besides, it was no new thing for the professional entertainer and laughter-maker to pretend to be something less than he was. Buffoons and parasites have made asses of themselves to amuse their hosts ever since Philippus took his uninvited place at the banquet described by Xenophon in his *Symposium* (II, 21 ff.).[30] It is no wonder then that the wandering minstrels and jesters of the early middle ages were willing to assume the guise of innocents and naturals. The merging of the professional jester with the licensed fool gave rise to a new species—the artificial fool or court jester. The fusion must have taken place as early as the twelfth century, for at that time a distinction already was being drawn between "natural fools" and "fools artificial" (Welsford, p. 119). And it was this artificial fool of tradition who was to grow eventually into the wise and witty fool of Shakespeare's plays.

The fool of tradition, however, was something more than a humorous entertainer; he was also the licensed critic of his master and his fellows. Since he was not held accountable for what his tongue wagged, the fool might clatter or speak unwelcome truths with comparative impunity. When he was whipped, as he occasionally was when he carried his impudence too far, he was chastised as a naughty child might be. Usually, however, his remarks were ignored or laughed at as mere babbling nonsense. For example, the rascally servant Piston, of *Soliman and Perseda* (1589–92), barely escapes imprisonment for rifling a corpse by feigning feeble-mindedness:

PHILIP. Say, villaine, wherefore didst thou rifle him?
PISTON. Faith, sir, for pure good will; seeing he was going towards heauen, I thought to see if he had a pasport to *S. Nicholas* or no.
PHILIP. Some sot he seems to be; twere pittie to hurt him. Sirra, canst thou tell who slew this man?
PISTON. I, sir, very well; it was my maister *Erastus*.
PHILIP. Thy maister? and whether is he gone now?
PISTON. To fetch the Sexten to bury him, I thinke.
PHILIP. Twere pittie to imprison such a sot.
PISTON. Now it fits my wisdome to counterfeit the foole.[31]

Even when the fool's random comments hit home, his fellows remark sententiously that "the fool tells true"[32] or that "This foole here hath got sum wyt,"[33] as if his wisdom were naive and purely accidental. Of her followers, the wise Moria observes:

And yet we se, that of fooles oftetymes, not onely true tales, but euin open rebukes are with pleasure declared. That what woorde comyng out of a wisemans mouthe were an hanging mattier, the same yet spoken by a foole shall muche delight euin him that is touched ther with.[34]

According to the tradition, the fool was often painfully candid. "Children & fooles they say can not l[y],"[35] runs the old proverb, and the trait sometimes amused and sometimes embarrassed his betters. If the fool was imprudently outspoken, he was so because he could not help himself, comments Moria.

For what soever he hath in his thought, that sheweth he also in his countinaunce, and expresseth it in hys talke. (*The Praise of Folie*, sig. G2ᵛ)

The female fool Lomia betrays the rascally Vice Common Conditions because she knows not how to tell an untruth.[36] And the counterfeit fools Will Summers and Passarello insist that they have not the wit to be flatterers.

Critics have spoken the blunt truth and shamed authority in all ages, but the professed fool exercised the privilege with less risk of reprisal. In ancient times, professional buffoons and parasites sometimes used a license somewhat akin to that allowed to the later court fool. Cleisophus, parasite to King Philip of Macedon, must have enjoyed an immunity like unto the fool's, if we can believe the anecdote told by Lynceus:

"Once Philip gave him [Cleisophus] a damaged horse, which he sold. And when, after a while, he was asked by the king where the horse was, he said, 'It's been sold for damages.' And when Philip, amid loud applause, perpetrated a joke at his expense, he said, 'After that, ought *I* not to be the one to keep *you*?' "[37]

In suggesting that the king change places with the jester, Cleisophus certainly anticipates some later court fools, especially the Fool in *Lear*. Lucian, in his *Lapithae* 19 (Fowler, iv, 134), describes an encounter between the cynic Alcidamas and the clown Satyrion, in which the philosopher comes off second best. Of course, one must allow for Lucian's bias wherever cynic philosophers are concerned.

The typical buffoon, with his crude jests and shrewd evasions, was never a notable truth-teller. But the poet and philosopher, as Doran suggests, sometimes told disagreeable truths to the tyrants of antiquity.[38] Although it is a far cry from the currish snarling of a Diogenes to the bantering humor of the wise court fool, the cynic spoke with a freedom and candor rarely found in the entourage of Alexander. Plutarch is our authority for the story of Alexander's meeting with Diogenes. Annoyed that the cynic had not joined the many statesmen and philosophers in congratulating him on his proposed expedition against Persia, Alexander sought out Diogenes in the suburb of Craneion.

When *Diogenes* saw so many coming towardes him, he sate up a litle, and looked full apon *Alexander*. *Alexander* courteously spake unto him, and asked him, if he lacked any thinge. Yea said he, that I do: that thou stand out of my sunne a litle. *Alexander* was so well pleased with this aunswere, and marvelled so much at the great boldnes of this man, to se how small account he made of him: that when he went his way from him, *Alexanders* familliers laughing at *Diogenes*, and mocking him, he told them: masters say what you lyst, truely if I were not *Alexander*, I would be *Diogenes*.[39]

The tale has been much augmented in the telling until in Lyly' play *Campaspe* (1584), Diogenes emerges as a severe critic of all kings.

ALEX. How happen it that you woulde not come out of your tub to my palace?
DIOG. Because it was as far from my tub to your pallace as from your palace to my tub.
ALEX. Why then, doest thou ow no reuerence to kings?
DIOG. No.
ALEX. Why so?
DIOG. Because they be no gods.
ALEX. They be gods of the earth.
DIOG. Yea, gods of earth. (II, ii, 192)[40]

Later in the play, Alexander again toys with the surly wit of the philosopher much as a later king would amuse himself with the pleasantries of his favorite fool:

ALEX. If thou mightest haue thy wil, how much ground would content thee?
DIOG. As much as you in the ende must be contented withall.
ALEX. What? a world?
DIOG. No; the length of my body. (V, iv, 78)

In the acrid taste of his wit, Diogenes suggests Thersites rather than Touchstone, but he does, like the traditional fool, use a license to speak blunt truths and correct folly.

Other ancient philosophers have not always fared so well as did Diogenes. Anaxarchus, a favorite of Alexander's, earned the enmity of

Nicocreon, king of Cyprus. After the death of Alexander, Anaxarchus fell into the hands of Nicocreon, who promptly put him to a most cruel death. As he was being pounded to pulp in a huge mortar, Anaxarchus exhorted his executioners: "Pound, pound the pouch containing Anaxarchus; ye pound not Anaxarchus." For his defiance, Nicocreon threatened to cut out the philosopher's saucy tongue. Whereupon Anaxarchus showed his vast contempt for the barbarous tyrant by biting his tongue in two and spitting out the mangled piece in the face of Nicocreon.[41] The story is probably apocryphal, but it does illustrate how freely some philosophers used their tongues.

But in ancient Attica, the comic poets most freely indulged in bold and merry repartee. During the Lenaean festivals when their comedies were produced and entered for prizes, the dramatists apparently enjoyed a special license to be ribald and to lampoon the great men of the city—two privileges which the later court fools were to exercise. Dicaeopolis, in *The Acharnians* (425 B.C.), justifies his plain speaking as a right derived from the Dionysian celebration:

> Bear me no grudge, spectators, if, a beggar,
> I dare to speak before the Athenian people
> About the city in a comic play.
> For what is true even comedy can tell.
> And I shall utter startling things but true.
> Nor now can Cleon slander me because,
> With strangers present, I defame the State.
> 'Tis the Lenaea, and we're all alone . . .[42]

That impudent satirist Aristophanes must have grinned when in the debate between Right Reason and Wrong Reason, in *The Clouds* (423 B.C.), both disputants vie with one another in reviling the lawyers, the tragic poets, the demagogues, and even the members of the audience (ll. 1088–1100). The liberty which these figures take in railing on the people of Athens is very like the fool's prerogative to satirize the king and courtiers of a later day. The comic poet himself assumes the role of truth-speaker in the parabasis, or middle portion, of *The Acharnians*. Aristophanes, with none of the fool's mock-modesty, describes himself as "the poet so fearless and witty, / Who dared in the presence of Athens to speak the thing that is rightful and true" (ll. 644–645).

But although the comic poet often took upon himself the role of licensed critic, he sometimes relegated this responsibility to one of the characters in his play. For example, after Dicaeopolis has made his separate peace with the Spartan enemy, he is accused of naive blundering and even of treason by the chorus of super-patriotic charcoal-burners. He answers them with disarming directness:

> Yet I know that these our foemen,
> who our bitter wrath excite,
> Were not always wrong entirely,
> nor ourselves entirely right. (ll. 309–310)

Later on he points to the "grey-haired veterans in the ranks" and the "paltry malingering boys" as evidence that the Peloponnesian War had already gone on long enough (ll. 600–601). But voicing such unpopular truths brings no citation for contempt of the Athenian *prytanes* upon Dicaeopolis.

The wise fool of our study was not always so blunt in his truth-telling or so direct in his ridiculing of folly as was the philosopher or the poet. And unlike the typical buffoon, he was more often ironical than scurrilous in his critical comments. The difference between these spokesmen was essentially a difference in temper and tone. Irony of manner is as old as the comic spirit and one of its earliest manifestations. Like the idea of buffoonery and pretentious folly, the idea of irony finds its first expression in the behavior of a comic character of the Greek stage—the εἴρων or ironical man.[43] Originally the εἴρων was a crafty individual who specialized in understatement. He was quite ready to appear the fool, to mask his voice in a thick dialect, if in so doing he could take in the ἀλαζών or bragging impostor.[44] Of course, the traditional fool, even of the artificial variety, had little in common with this sly, foxy fellow. The fool, as we have already noted, was essentially a truthful person. If he disguised his true wits under a fool's cap and bells, he did so in order that he might speak the truth more freely and more fearlessly.

The witty fool of renaissance tradition finds his classical counterpart in the mocking philosopher of the Platonic *Dialogues*. Socrates, in accepting and appropriating to himself the ill-natured slurs of Alcibiades and Thrasymachus, transforms the meaning of irony and refines upon the character of the ironical man.[45] In a more generous mood, Alcibiades aptly describes the ironical philosopher:

> . . . he is exactly like the busts of Silenus, which are set up in the statuaries' shops, holding pipes and flutes in their mouths; and they are made to open in the middle, and have images of gods inside them . . . his outer mask is the carved head of the Silenus; but, O my companions in drink, when he is opened, what temperance there is residing within![46]

But Thrasymachus mistakes Socrates' profession of ignorance for insincerity, his genuine humility for mock-modesty.

Thrasymachus, I [Socrates] said, with a quiver, don't be hard upon us. Polemarchus and I may have been guilty of a little mistake in the argument, but I can assure you that the error was not intentional . . . And why, when we are seeking for justice, a thing more precious than many pieces of gold, do you say that we are weakly yielding to one another and not doing our utmost to get at the truth? Nay, my good friend, we are most willing and anxious to do so, but the fact is that we cannot. And if so, you people who know all things should pity us and not be angry with us.

How characteristic of Socrates! he [Thrasymachus] replied, with a bitter laugh; —that's your ironical style! Did I not foresee—have I not already told you, that whatever he was asked he would refuse to answer, and try irony or any other shuffle, in order that he might avoid answering? (*Republic* i, 336–7)

But Socrates uses rhetorical irony often, not as a shuffle or an evasion but to correct the folly of presumption in others and to get at the truth. Like the cruder *εἴρων* of Dorian comedy, Socrates delights in tripping up his boastful assailants.

Happy is Evenus, I [Socrates] said to myself, if he really has this wisdom, and teaches at such a moderate charge. Had I the same, I should have been very proud and conceited; but the truth is that I have no knowledge of the kind. (*Apology* 20d)

For Socrates, self-depreciation is not merely a pose, as it is for Thrasymachus or for Critias, but a truly humble attitude toward himself and toward the results of his reasoning. He shows himself a wise fool in the same sense in which Saint Paul and Erasmus were later to use the epithet.

You see then, Critias, that I was not far wrong in fearing that I could have no sound notion about wisdom; I was quite right in depreciating myself. . . . I would rather advise you to regard me simply as a fool who is never able to reason out anything; and to rest assured that the more wise and temperate you are, the happier you will be. (*Charmides* 175–176)

To liken the fool of tradition to the great humanist philosopher may seem to be painting too high a brow upon the features of the far cruder and less complex man in motley. But the likeness is there, nevertheless. And when we come to look at some of Shakespeare's wise and witty fools, the similarity will become more apparent.

Erasmus' panegyric on Folly provides a possible link between the irony of Socrates and the gay insouciance of the renaissance fool. In the person of Moria and her followers, several incongruities in the fool tradition meet and are merged. She pays homage to the noble Athenian, who "in one pointe (me semeth) was not all wise, in that he woulde not take upon him the name of a wiseman, but rather ascribed the same unto god onely . . ." (*The praise of Folie, sig.* D3^{v}). She numbers in her train those idle, vain, and vicious fools who had earlier crowded the decks of Brandt's *Narrenschiff* and Barclay's *The Ship of Foles.*[47] But she reserves her real love for that "kinde of men, whome commenly ye call fooles, doltes, ideotes, and paches" (sig. G^{v}). These innocent fools, Moria contends, are the only truly happy creatures:

> . . . These my selie paches. Who not onelye them selues are euer mery, playing, singing, and laughynge: but also whateuer they doo, are prouoker of others lykewyse to pleasure, sporte, and laughter . . . (sig. G2).

Sometimes these fools are nourished in their happiness by a benevolent ignorance or a delightful delusion. At other times they joy in a supernal wisdom that goes deeper than reason may plumb.

Everything is grist to Moria's mill, and she mixes the meal with the chaff indiscriminately. She finds matter to feed on in the pagan writers, Horace, Homer, and Cicero, and in the sacred authors, Solomon, Saint Paul, and Ecclesiasticus. A sample of the way in which she turns blame into praise of Folly may be seen from her comments on the preacher's words in Ecclesiastes: "The heart of the wise is in the house of mourning; but the heart of fools is in the house of mirth" (vii, 4). This, Moria contends, is an open confession that nothing in life is sweet without the admixture of folly and that to have learned wisdom is not enough if one does not add to it an understanding of folly. From the same text, she observes that the Preacher applied his heart "to know wisdom, and to know madness and folly," in that order. She conveniently forgets to finish the quotation: ". . . this also was a striving after wind" (*Eccl.* i, 17). Of course, such an argument is pure quibbling, but then there is nothing dearer to the heart of Moria or the stage fool. Shakespeare's Feste and Lavache are adepts at quibbles and chop-logic.

In her rambling discourse, Moria mixes matter and impertinency in about the same proportions as we find them in the speeches of her devotees —the professional fools of the court and the stage. If we may judge from Holbein's illustration of Moria haranguing her foolish auditors, she wears the usual garb of the professional jester, and a pair of Midas-ears peeps from beneath the doctoral cowl that she has put on for the occasion.[48] At least her words suggest this appearance:

On all sydes I dooe resemble my selfe. So that not so muche as they can dissemble me, who take upon theim most semblante of wisdome, and walke lyke Asses in Lyons skynnes. That althoughe they counterfeite what they can, yet on some syde their longe eares pearyng foorth, doe discouer them to come of Midas progenie. (Chaloner ed., sig. A3)

Moria uses the fool's traditional license to comment on folly, whether in kings or commoners, popes or parish priests. She also echoes the gnomic wisdom of the people in remarking that: "*It is most wysedome for a man in place to countrefaicte Folie*" (sig. Q^v).

In these many ways, the wise Moria follows and continues the fool of tradition. However, there is a respect in which she refines upon this typical fool. Omnipresent in her speech is the sense of comic irony:

One man see they redie to die for loue of a woman, and the lesse he is beloued, the more hotely to pursue hir . . . (sig. K2^v)

. . . .

. . . they [Dunsmen] descriue and peyncte unto us all thinges doone in hell, so exactly as if many yeres they had soiourned in the diuels court. (sig. M4)

. . . .

. . . armed onely with *thre sillogismes*, thei [lawyers] dare boldely prouoke any man. (sig. L3^v)

. . . .

. . . learned men, who in hope of promocion, will name and expounde this theyr open madnesse to be Zeale, to be a Pietie, to bee a Spiritual manhode in them, bringing it by a new foũd meanes to passe, that now a man may thrust his sword into his brothers bealye, obseruing neuertheless that loue and perfite charitie whiche Christe byddeth eche Christian to owe an other. (sig. P3)

We need not multiply instances further; irony runs like a golden thread throughout the tangled skein of Moria's argument. But the irony that she uses is not merely a rhetorical trope or a verbal felicity; it is her characteristic manner, her way of looking at life and the people about her. In one breath she ironically praises those vain and vicious persons who excel in the ways of the world; in another, she commends those simple souls whose folly is brighter far than the dull wisdom of earth. Her commonwealth is coextensive with the world. In his *The Praise of Folly*, Erasmus filled in the features of the wise, ironical fool; it remained for Shakespeare to bring this fool to the Elizabethan stage.

Chapter II. EMERGENCE OF THE STAGE FOOL

To recognize that Feste, Touchstone, and Lear's Fool come near the close of a great popular and literary tradition takes nothing from Shakespeare's invention. Without this tradition reaching back into classical and medieval times the wise fools of Erasmus and Shakespeare might never have been. Touchstone was the first truly wise fool to caper and tumble across the Elizabethan stage. But before him a whole host of vain and vicious fools swarmed forth to frolic in the French *sotties* and the Tudor moral plays. These knavish fools and jesting Vices sometimes wore the habitual garb of the court fool. Cap and bells first made their appearance on the French stage in the *sotties* or farces of Adam de la Halle during the latter half of the thirteenth century. One of these, *Le Jeu de la Feuillée* (c. 1276), is a delightful blend of village realism and fairyland fantasy, but the fools of the piece resemble the clowns of *A Midsummer Night's Dream* far more than they do the ironical jesters of Arden and Illyria. The playlets of Adam de la Halle clearly are fool plays, and yet they antedate by more than one hundred years the next works in this genre. The later *sottie* grew out of the celebrations of the ecclesiastical "Feast of Fools" and the secular *Sociétés Joyeuses*.[1] All those who participated put on the traditional motley, eared hood, bells and bauble and annually elected a Prince of Sots or *Mère-Folle* to rule over the festivities. The society sought refuge in the masquerade of fools to snipe covertly at the political and ecclesiastical follies of the day.

Because of the essentially satirical cast of these plays, the knaves and fools of this world are represented by players in motley. They are akin to the crew assembled by Brandt and Barclay and to the inmates of Garzoni's spital house. The braggart and the learned impostor, those immemorial butts of the comic spirit, are here decked out in fool's regalia. We will look in vain for anyone like the witty fool of Elizabethan drama unless it be the character of *Mère-Folle* herself. She is the mother of this vast brood of knaves and ninnies, and she alternately nurtures and mocks them in a manner which may have given Erasmus a hint for his Moria. A new figure sometimes appears in the *sotties* of the sixteenth century. He does not wear motley and by common consent he is neither a sot nor a sage but the *badin*, who "Knows more of honor or of goodness / Than a fool may learn in all his life."[2] This buffoon is closer in spirit to the witty fools and clever clowns of the Elizabethan stage than are his fellows in motley. He is the ironical bystander or commentator. In one of these later plays, the *badin* serves as comic chorus and calls the roll of fools and impostors. In addition to the usual blustering braggarts and pedants who so often come in for ridicule, he also notes: "That the fools who have the name of subtle / And ingenious are really ridiculous / And full of amusing diversion. / They find such depths to their own intellects / That if one were to credit their writings / He would think that they were first cousins to God."[3] This nimble-witted *badin* is a true precursor to Shakespeare's wise fool, but if there is any direct connection between the two, the link must be in Erasmus, who was familiar with the French theatre.

In Germany, the *Fastnachtspiele*, or Carnival plays presented at Shrovetide, are the equivalent of the French *sottie*. Using a similar license, these little plays are quite as satirical as the French fool plays; the doctrine that *Stultorum infinitus est numerus* again finds expression throughout. The *Narr*, like the French sot, wears an eared hood and he is a standard figure in most Carnival plays. However, there is no German counterpart to *Mère-Folle* or *badin* to act as commentator and to unmask the fools. Instead, the *Narren* convict themselves of folly in quite undramatic fashion and without a trace of irony. An exception to this rule may be found in the play or plays based upon the Solomon-Marcolf dialogues. C. H. Herford mentions a Carnival play entitled *Marcolfus* which was performed in Lucerne in 1546.[4] Dr. A. von Keller, however, includes an earlier *Ein Spil von König Salomon und Markolfo* in his edition of fifteenth century *Fastnachtspiele*. Here, as in the original Latin *Collationes*, a boorish buffoon outwits the sage Solomon. Marcolf's cynical, worldly maxims serve as a counterpoise to the pretentious platitudes of Solomon. His debased view of women reappears again and again in later fool literature. Even Erasmus, whose Moria is a woman, indulges in the popular satire on women and lechery. There is also something of the slippery rogue in Marcolf as in that other German trickster Til Eulenspiegel. Many of his witty shifts are merely tricks to escape punishment or hanging.

What interests us most is not Marcolf's crude jests or his foul-mouthed railing but the fact that this rustic lout impudently reproves the king for his foolish vanity:

SALOMON. God gave us wisdom and skill so that none might be like us in all the kingdom.

MARCOLF. He who has unpleasant neighbors must praise himself.[5]

And in another place, Marcolf replies to the king's boasting: "He is wise who believes himself to be a fool."[6] This reversal of roles in which the apparently wise man changes places with the fool is the very essence of comic irony. Lear's Fool with a similar show of impudent wit suggests that his master wear his coxcomb (*Lear* I, iv, 121). This German playlet on *Salomon und Markolfo* is interesting also in that it first presents Marcolf in motley and thereby anticipates Birck's *Sapientia Solomonis*, a mid-sixteenth century Elizabethan play in Latin.

When we cross the Channel, we find a very different development of the fool in drama. The English church countenanced no such indecorous or Saturnalian celebrations as the Feast of Fools. Nor were there any permanent confraternities of young bohemians similar to the continental *Enfants-sans-souci*. As a consequence, the English had no fool plays of a satirical sort comparable to the French *sottie* or the German Carnival play. Instead, we find that the fool of tradition had become merged in the character of the comic Vice of the Tudor moral play, his trait of ironical jesting having interfused with other, less commendable features. And it is this trait of irony which the Vice chiefly passed on to the later stage fool. This character was not labelled "the Vice" until the time of John Heywood, but from his various names—Hypocrisy, Idleness, Mischief, or Sensuality—we may conjecture on his descent from the Seven Deadly Sins of the homilies. In the older plays he came on the stage or pageant in the Devil's retinue, but at some point in his stage career he became the antagonist of the Devil and belabored him with his wooden lath. Sinne, for example, teases and taunts Satan in Thomas Lupton's *All For Money* (c. 1558). However, at the end of the typical moral play, the Vice climbs on the Devil's shoulders and rides off pickaback to Hell.[7]

So complete was the confusion between the jesting Vice and the stage fool at one time that the jester Richard Tarleton was sometimes referred to as the Vice. Feste is evidently aware of his descent from the "old Vice" and of his ancient enmity with the Devil if we may judge by the jingling rhyme with which he takes his leave of Malvolio:

> I am gone, sir;
> And anon, sir,
> I'll be with you again,
> In a trice,
> Like to the old Vice,
> Your need to sustain;
> Who, with dagger of lath,
> In his rage and his wrath,

Cries 'aha!' to the devil.
Like a mad lad,
'Pare thy nails, dad.'
Adieu, goodman devil. (*Twel.* IV, ii, 130)

One needs to see a parallel between the two sets of roles to fully appreciate the mockery in Feste's comment.

L. W. Cushman, in his study of the Devil and the Vice, denies that any relationship exists between the mocking Vice of the morality and the traditional figure of the fool.[8] He stresses the allegorical nature of the Vice's role as an embodiment of one of the Seven Deadly Sins. Although this aspect of his role needs to be remembered, it is no more important from a theatrical standpoint than is his function as mirth-maker in the play. As a mirth-maker, whose range is from rough horseplay to ironical commentary, the Vice of the Tudor interlude has something in common with the sots and *Mère-Folle* of the French farce. Each of these theatrical types begins as a representation of an abstract vice or folly; each develops or deteriorates, depending upon your point of view, into a buffoonish character who carries on the main comic business of the play. Knave though he be, the comic Vice is not humorless. For his mocking humor, not his knavery, he interests us as a forerunner of the Elizabethan stage fool.

We may as well concede a point to Cushman at the beginning. There is no conclusive evidence from the extant plays that the jesting Vice always wore motley on the stage. Ignorance, a secondary Vice to Idleness in John Redford's allegorical interlude *Wyt and Science* (c. 1530), does wear the fool's coat and coxcomb, but Ignorance is no witty jester. Later in the play, Wyt appears in the garb of Ignorance and is taken "for no naturall foole, / Browght up among the innocentes scoole, / But for a nawgty vycious foole, / Browght up wyth Idellnes in her scoole" (ll. 784–787).[9] Another "nawgty vycious foole" is the character Moros from Wager's morality *The longer thou liuest, the more foole thou art* (c. 1559). Moros is an impious knave who at the close of the play is given a fool's coat and a sharp rebuke by Gods Judgment for his willful folly. But Moros fulfills the role of Youth or Everyman misled by vice rather than the part of Vice itself. And it is Wrath, one of the Seven Deadly Sins and no fool, who ironically comments upon Moros as the latter tries to read a book: "Alas, one worde to reade in it he is not able. / More fooles then he, to geue him a booke. / A foole will delight more in a bable, / And more mete for him theron to looke" (ll. 754–757).[10]

Certainly, if the wearing of motley were the only measure, then there is little evidence of a fusion or confusion of the fool with the comic Vice on the stage.

Fortunately our argument for the identity of the fool and the Vice does not hang upon the costumes they wore. The comic Vice has in common with his offspring, the later stage fool, a witty, ironical disposition. Both characters often act as commentators and occasionally as satirical spokesmen. The "vyce" Merry-Report, in John Heywood's *The Play of the Wether* (1533), resembles a court jester in his behavior even if he does not necessarily wear the conventional garb. His tone of light-hearted merriment and banter is tipped now and again with acid. Merry-Report rebukes the two millers for their needless quarreling. He answers the coarse railing of the laundress in kind. And the pretty but vain gentlewoman he lovingly chaffs even as he flirts with her. Heywood's other Vice, Neither-Lover-Nor-Loved in his *Play of Love* (1534), comes running on stage with burning squibs popping about him. The fireworks were part of the standard equipment of the green man of the Lord Mayor's Show rather than of the traditional fool or Vice. But this Vice resembles the stage fool in other ways. His little Chaucerian anecdote about the lady who protested her faithfulness too much tends to discredit the fulsome declarations of the three lover types. It serves as a comment on the rest of the action of the play much as Touchstone's tale of wooing Jane Smile does in his play.

The comic Vice has in common with most fun-makers his bag of stock tricks and stage by-play. Among his verbal shifts and devices are the distorted echo, mistaking the word, comic stichomythia, innuendo, stage asides, and parody. Some of these fetches do not concern us as they are in no way related to the development of the stage fool. Mistaking the word is a trick as old as Aristophanes and as recent as the latest Fibber McGee show. Shakespeare gives this comic business mostly to such clowns as Dogberry and Mistress Quickly, not to his wise fools. The distorted echo occurs in the *Croxton Play of the Sacrament* (1468), wherein Colle, a clever servant not a comic Vice, exposes his master Brundyche as a quack-doctor who kills more than he cures. But though this device is part of the standard stage business in many Elizabethan plays, it seldom serves any critical purpose. Mocking criticism and ridicule of folly are best expressed through innuendo, stage asides, comic stichomythia, and direct parody; and the Vice shows himself the father of the stage fool in his predilection to these.

The convention of the comic aside is a rather ironical means to mock a person and ridicule his behavior. The crafty Vice Hypocrisy in Woodes' *The Conflict of Conscience* (c. 1570) uses this trick to comment slyly on his fellow Vices and erstwhile cronies, Avarice and Tyranny.

AVAR. In faith if I thought that he might bee spared,
And we haue our purpose beshrew mee if I cared.
HYPOC. Your kind hart shal cost me a couple of russhes. (ll. 433–435)[11]

In a like manner, the Vice Inclination in *The Trial of Treasure* (c. 1567) girds at his fellows:

TREAS. Both trusty and true ye shall me alwayes finde.
INCL. As trusty as is a quicke ele by the tayle.[12]

Common as this stage convention is, few professional fools make use of it. The fool, as we have already observed, enjoys a special license to speak his mind freely. If he has reason to fear the whip for his impudence, he sometimes disguises his meaning or lapses into apparent nonsense as Lear's Fool does. In either circumstance, he has little need for the stage whisper or the comic aside.

In his use of innuendo and verbal irony, the jesting Vice most nearly resembles the fool of tradition. Sinne, in Lupton's rather crude *All For Money*, is more knave than fool, wise or otherwise. However, he does manage some satirical gibes at the fraudulent claimants and suitors to Money. Here he mocks Gregorie Graceles, who brags that he "can cut a mans purse and looke in his face":

SINNE. If your personage be as handsome as your qualities be good,
The hempe for your hanging beginnes for to budde. (ll. 1024–1028)

He jeers at an amorous old crone in a manner that recalls the *Ecclesiazusae* of Aristophanes:

Goope with a gaulde backe come vp to supper,
Gylle my olde mare must haue a newe crupper:
A meeter mariage then this did I neuer see,
For she is not past four score yeres elder then he (ll. 1365–1368)

. . . .

Do you see yonder, olde mother Croote
would as fayne be trode as a yonger pullet:
Howe will her husband do when he should kisse her,
Her nose and her chinne meetes almost together.
Oh, she wilbe a trimme bryde that day she is wedde,
One would thinke she smyled if her teeth were in her head. (ll. 1396–1402)

Before we too hastily censure Thomas Lupton for raising a laugh at the expense of age and ugliness, we should remember what Fielding says on the subject of affectation: "when ugliness aims at the applause of beauty, or lameness endeavors to display agility, it is then that these unfortunate circumstances, which at first moved our compassion, tend only to raise our mirth."[13]

Akin to the mimicry of the distorted echo is the use of a kind of comic stichomythia, wherein the Vice-fool matches his opposite, sentence for grave sentence and proverb for proverb. This is the technique of the dialogues of Solomon and Marcolf, of Heywood's debate between *Witty and Witless*. Hardy Dardy, in *Godly Queen Hester* (?1525–1529), uses comic stichomythia to confound the arguments of Aman:

AMAN. Fooles largely will bourde and tell al theyr thought.
HARDY. And wyse men will not speke one worde till all become to nought
AMAN. Fooles will tell all and that trobleth sore,
HARDY. And wyse men will say nought at al till al be gone & more
AMAN. Fooles to Idlenes all wayes be preste.
HARDY. And wyse men vse such busines it were better they were at rest
AMAN. Fooles let the reformation, of commonwele.
HARDY. And wyse men be so full of imaginacion they wot not how they deale.
AMAN. Whyse men wolde do ryght, And foles say nay.
HARDY. And fooles be fayne to fyght when wise men rūne away. (ll. 664–673)[14]

Is Lear's Fool echoing this last line when he declares his loyalty to his master (*Lear* II, iv, 83)?

If Greg is right in assigning so early a date as 1525–1529 to the production of this Biblical play,[15] then we have in Hardy Dardy the first representation of a consistently ironical jester on the English stage. Although he is labelled "a vice" in the Dramatis Personae, that designation is a misnomer as it was when applied to Heywood's Merry-Report. Hardy Dardy is more nearly a wise fool than are such ambiguous figures as Ralph Simnell, Cacurgus, or the later Marcolf. He exhibits a certain prophetic sense found in some later wise fools. He predicts Aman's hanging on the gallows designed for Mardocheus. Later he points up the irony of the situation by retelling an old fable of King Phalaris and the bull of brass. To King Assuerus' query about his meaning, Hardy Dardy replies: "I mean my master is the fyrst taster, of his owne inuencion. / The gallhouse he made both hye and brode, / For Mardocheus he them mente, / And now he is faine him selfe for certaine, / To play the fyrst pagente" (ll. 1047–1052). By wittily ridiculing the folly in others yet not boasting of his own wisdom, Hardy Dardy places himself in the company of wise fools of Erasmus, Grimald, and Shakespeare.

Although the jesting Vice, like the fool, sometimes acts as a satirical commentator, he behaves also like the witty fool when he mocks his victims through parody. Mischief, the Vice of *Mankind* (c. 1475), with his attendant imps, Nought, New-Gyse, and Now-A-Days, pokes fun at the pedantic Mercy with his satchel full of "Englysch Laten":

MERCY. The corn xall be sauyde, the chaffe xall be brente.
I be-sech yow hertyly, haue this premedytacyon.
[Enter Mischief.]
MYSCHEFFE. I be-seche yow hertyly, leue yowur calcacyon!
Leue yowur chaffe! leue yowur corn! leue yowur dalyacyon!
Yowur wytt ys lytyll, yowur hede ys mekyll! ye are full of predycacyon.
But, ser, I prey [yow] this questyon to claryfye:–
Dryff-draff, mysse-masche,
Sume was corn, and sume was chaffe;
My dame seyde my name was Raffe;
On-schett yowur lokke, and take an halpenye.
MERCY. Why come ye hethyr, brother?
Ye were not dysyryde.
MYSCHEFFE. For a wyntur corn-threscher, ser, I haue hyryde;
Ande ye sayde the corn xulde be sauyde, and the chaffe xulde be feryde;
Ande he prouyth nay, as yt schewth be this werse: "Corn seruit bredibus, chaffe horsibus, straw fyrybusque,"
Thys ys as moche to say to yowur leude wndyrstondynge,
As the corn xall serue to brede at the nexte bakynge,
"Chaff horsybus," *et reliqua,*
The chaff, to horse xall be goode produce;
When a man ys for-colde, this straw may be brent.
And so forth, *et cetera.* (ll. 43–63)[16]

Critics have long noted the clever parody of aureate language and "halff chongyd Latyne"[17] in passages such as this. Equally noteworthy is the fact that the shrewd, mundane wisdom of Mischief is more than a match for the platitudinizing of Mercy.

The motley-minded gentlemen in the moral plays after the middle of the sixteenth century show a great diminution of wit. *Lusty Juventus* (c. 1548/9) has a mocking Vice, Hypocrisy, who is occasionally witty if not very wise. He scoffs at Juventus' pious pedantry much as Mischief had jeered at Mercy's affectation in *Mankind.* When Hypocrisy goes on to berate "The foule presumptions of youth,"[18] we can almost hear

Falstaff speaking—the Falstaff whom Prince Hal stigmatizes as "that reverend vice, that grey iniquity" (*I H. IV* II, iv, 500). Haphazard, a prankster and a turncoat, is partially responsible for the complications of the plot in *Apius and Virginia* (1567/8). He has no redeeming quality unless it be his skill in lying and evasion. Subtle Shift, in the fantastical *Sir Clyomon and Sir Clamydes* (c. 1580), is called "the vice" in a stage direction, but he is a buffoonish servingman or parasite rather than a jester. As his name suggests, his chief skill is in extricating himself from awkward situations. He, too, is an intriguer, deeply involved in the plot of the play. So, too, is the mischievous Vice who gives his name to the play *Common Conditions* (c. 1576). More than that, he is the moving spirit of the play; the contriver of the plot. In this respect, Common Conditions foreshadows the wit-intriguers of Chapman's comedies. He holds in his hands the various threads of the plot, tangles them, and then unwinds them largely at his own convenience.

The exigencies of the role give Common Conditions an ambiguous character. He is as fickle as the fortunes of man and as inconstant as the wind. At one moment he is the nimble Vice misleading frail humanity, at the next he is the generous friend who brings lovers together, and then at a whim he is off again, perpetrating some new mischief. This whimsical side of his nature, coupled with his ability to render himself invisible, makes Common Conditions a prototype for Puck and the Merry Devil of Edmonton. In his own words, this slippery Vice is "neither fish nor flesh, but halfe a true knave, halfe a lier" (l. 112).[19] When he accompanies Sedmond and Clarissa into banishment, he seems to be a loyal-hearted fool like Babulo or Touchstone. But with his next prank or quirk of fortune, his goodness turns to pitch. Common Conditions then becomes the greedy parasite (ll. 728–729), who like his prototype in Roman comedy plots the intrigue of the play. His trick to escape the three murderous tinkers is of a piece with some of Marcolf's shifts. He reminds us of Marcolf and some other stage fools in his mouthing of old familiar proverbs, such as: "Hee that trusts to a broken bough, may hap to fall from the tree" (l. 557). As one who mimics romantic lovers, Common Conditions looks back to Neither-Lover-Nor-Loved and forward to Touchstone. He also presents us with the problem of disentangling the scheming Vice from the mocking jester. The exceptions, Merry-Report and Hardy Dardy, only prove the rule that the jesting Vice was a curious blend of intriguer against the good and a humorous, sometimes ironical commentator on the characters and action of the play. But the very nature of the role, the involvement of the Vice in the plot of the play, kept him from being the disinterested observer and critic that the wise fool so often is.

Long before the Vice had left the Elizabethan stage, regular fools in motley had already begun to appear. Cacurgus, the counterfeit fool of *Misogonus* (1560< >1577), is not the earliest of these fools, but he interests us because he illustrates the process of fusion or contamination working in reverse. Just as the jesting Vice in his composition unmistakably shows the influence of the fool of popular tradition, this stage fool clearly shows the counter-influence of the scheming Vice. As a wit-intriguer, a knave, and an impostor, Cacurgus resembles Jonson's Mosca and Face. Though he pretends to babbling lunacy before his old master, he unmasks himself in a soliloquy. He is a schemer and a scoundrel throughout the play, but like the typical Vice he does serve a critical function when he apes the manners of the profligate priest, Sir John. When Misogonus promises to make the fool his chaplain, Cacurgus thanks him and replies: "I could mumble my mattinges & durge wth the best . . ." (I, iii, 47). He also anticipates some later wise fools in his perception of the fool's paradoxical role: "a foole (quoth yow) nay he is no foole . . . he is able to sett your doctoures to schole" (I, ii, 19).

Skelton gives us a more satisfactory fusion of the intriguing Vice and the satirical fool in the person of Folly in *Magnyfycence* (c. 1516). In its preoccupation with political allegory and satire, this play shows kinship with the French comic morality and *sottie*. Its two fools, Fancy and Folly, one a natural, the other a counterfeit fool, are as sharply contrasted as the fools Patch and Will Summers must have been at the court of Henry VIII. Like the later coney-catching rogues of Greene and Jonson, Folly easily defrauds Fancy of his purse and then reads him a lecture: "Ha, ha, ha! herke, Syrs, harke! / For all that my name hyght Foly, / By the masse, yet art thou more fole than I" (l. 1110–1112). Of course, it requires little skill or wit to gull Fancy of his purse, but before we dismiss Folly as merely a scheming rogue, we ought to listen to him rail on the fool of presumption:

> I haue another maner of sorte
> That I laugh at for my dysporte;
> And those be they that come vp of nought,–
> As some be not ferre and yf it were well sought,–
> Such dawys, what soeuer they be,
> That be set in auctorite;
> Anone he waxyth so hy and prowde,
> He frownyth fyersly, brymly browde;
> The knaue wolde make it koy, and he cowde;
> All that he dothe muste be alowde;
> And, "This is not well done, Syr; take hede";

And maketh hym besy where is no nede;
He dawnsys so long, 'hey troly loly,'
That euery man lawghyth at his Foly. (ll. 1239–1252)

These lines would fit an upstart like Malvolio, but they were probably directed at Cardinal Wolsey. As he says of himself, Skelton's Folly is no fool, but a maker of fools. Like *Mère-Folle* and Erasmus' Moria, he is both a personification of human folly and at the same time a witty critic of fools.

Gallic influence is particularly noticeable in Sir David Lindsay's *Ane Satyre of the Thrie Estaitis.* This rather long moral play, performed before the Scottish Queen-Regent on 12 August 1554, shows definite traces of the *sottie*, both in its satirical design and in the traditional figure of Folly who emerges at the end. At first, Folly appears as a boorish clown who has just escaped from a tussle with an angry sow. But when he begins to dispense fools' hoods to the assorted knaves of the court and clergy, he clearly recalls *Mère-Folle.*[20] Folly has a hat for those insatiable merchant men who, not satisfied with normal profits, sail out on wintry seas against the Acts of Parliament to risk their lives and goods in the hope of greater gains. He offers fools' caps to those dotards of fourscore who marry young girls under fourteen. However, he reserves his greatest scorn for those hypocrite priests and imperial fools who hurt others with their folly:

This is ane haly Hude I say the.
This Hude is ordanit I the assure,
For Sprituall fuillis that taks in cure
The saullis of great Diosies,
And regiment of great Abesies,
For gredines of warldlie pelfe,
Than can nocht iustlie gyde them selfe.
Vthers sauls to saife it settis them weill,
Syne sell thair awin saullis to the Deuill. (ll. 4528–4536)

To those proud and greedy princes who think nothing of shedding the blood of their subjects to win themselves worldly power and glory, Folly contemptuously offers a hood with "luggis [ears] als lang as Muillis" (l. 4559).

Wise fools and jesters have their own set of tricks and devices as a part of their regular stage business. As we have just seen, the fool frequently offers his coxcomb and bauble to those whom he considers more foolish. One of the earliest instances of this gesture comes not from a play but from a quaint fifteenth century document known as "The Sage Fool's Testament." An old fool about to die makes the following disposition of his few worldly belongings:

I have lovyd so well your fadyr, that I Covett & Dessyre to be in hys Company Above all thyngis, for he lovyd me so well. And I know well that he ys in hell; wherfor I wolde be with hym. And I gyve to my lady your wyffe my Bedde, be Cawse that she myghte lye on hyt; for now she lyethe so softe, that hyt ys All-moste none or that she Ryse. And to your Steward, my hode; be Cawse hyt hathe iiij erys. for where ye put All your truste in hym, to pay your Credytour & the pore pepyll, he may not here. And to your Amner, my Babyll: Be Cawse when he delyveryth your Almys A-monge the pore pepull, they prese on hym, & thene he betis them with hys Staffe, that the Blode Ron Abowte there erys; & my babyll ys Softer.[21]

And we all remember how the Fool offers his coxcomb first to Kent and then to the King in Shakespeare's *Lear* (I, iv, 106).

Among the many kinds of parody and travesty which the fool indulges in, the mock-serious sermon is one of the most effective. At the close of Lindsay's *Ane Satyre*, Folly preaches a mock sermon on the text: *Stultorum numerus infinitus.*

To be ane fuill amang the laife,
Howbeit ane hundreth stands heir by,
Perventure als great fuillis as I.
Stultorum.
I haue of my Genelogie,
Dwelland in everie cuntrie,
Earles, Duiks, Kings, and Empriours,
With mony guckit Conquerours,
Quhilk dois in Folie perseveir,
And hes done sa this many year
Sum seiks to warldlie dignities,
And sum to sensuall vanities.
Quhat vails all thir vaine honour[i]s
Nocht being sure to leife twa houris?
Sum greidie fuill dois fill ane box:
Ane vther fuill cummis and breaks the lox,
And spends that vther fuillis hes spaird,
Quhilk never thocht on them to wairde.
Sum dois as thay sould never die.
Is nocht this folie, quhat say ye?
Sapientia huius mundi stultitia est apud Deum. (ll. 4472–4492)

Another amusing example of the mock-sermon appears in Grimald's Latin play *Archipropheta* (1547). Here Herod's fool, Gelasimus, exhorts his small congregation with the opening verses from Genesis and then goes on to expound:

GEL. The devil himself dwells in you, men and brothers, so overwhelmed with sin. Players abound in jokes, harlots in blandishments, games of chance in quarrels, the court in gossip, the market-places in lawsuits, feasts in whispering, and women in pride. This world is certainly most foul. Was there not darkness upon the face of the deep?
CHORUS. Ha, ha, ha!
SYR. GIRL. Ha, ha, ha!
GEL. Lest I should be too long-winded, I shall conclude with a story, or rather, with a sharply pointed little question: What seems to each one of you to be the most difficult thing to know? What do you think, what do you, and lastly, what do you? I certainly think it is, how one is to know his own father. What is a patriarch, a patriarch? And what is a fool, a fool? What is a woman? What, indeed, save a vain thing? And the spirit of the Lord moved upon the face of the waters. (II, ix, 17)[22]

This type of parody obviously derives from the French *sermons joyeux* of the late fifteenth or early sixteenth century.[23]

Shakespeare echoes this traditional form of parody, but as ever with a difference. Feste in the frock of Sir Topas exorcises the Devil in Malvolio and then delivers a brief homily:

MAL. I am not mad, Sir Topas. I say to you this house is dark.
CLOWN. Madman, thou errest. I say there is no darkness but ignorance, in which thou art more puzzled than the Egyptians in their fog. (*Twel.* IV, ii, 44)

Lavache discourses in a similar vein in reply to Lafeu:

I am a woodland fellow, sir, that always loved a great fire; and the master I speak of ever keeps a good fire. But sure he is the prince of the world; let his nobility remain in's court. I am for the house with the narrow gate, which I take to be too little for pomp to enter. Some that humble themselves may; but the many will be too chill and tender, and they'll be for the flow'ry way that leads to the broad gate and the great fire. (*All's W.* IV, v, 49)

A favorite trick of the old Vice and the later jester is to speak of himself as a personification of worldly vice and folly and make verbal play out of this confusion. As we have just seen, Folly in *Ane Satyre* preaches a

mock-sermon in which he identifies himself with the element of folly in others: "Earles, Duiks, Kings, and Empriours, / With mony guckit Conquerours, / Quhilk dois in Folie perseveir, / And hes done sa this many yeir" (ll. 4478–4481). An earlier instance of this device occurs in Skelton's morality, when Folly disabuses Crafty Conueyaunce of a false notion:

> CRA. CON. And for a fole a man wolde hym take.
> FOLIE. Nay, it is I that foles can make;
> For be he cayser or be he kynge,
> To felowshyp with Foly I can hym brynge.
> (*Magnyfycence*, ll. 1213–1216)

Passarello plays upon this ambiguity when he observes: "I am as common in the Court as an hostesses lippes in the countrey; knights, and clownes, and knaves, and all share mee: The Court cannot possibly be without me" (*Malc.* I, vii, 149). And Lavache, joking with Parolles, makes clever use of this equivocation:

> PAR. Go to, thou art a witty fool! I have found thee.
> CLOWN. Did you find me in yourself, sir, or were you taught to find me? The search, sir, was profitable; and much fool may you find in you, even to the world's pleasure and the increase of laughter. (*All's W.* II, iv, 32)

But Feste plays most wittily with this trick of verbal confusion. He manages to combine a wry comment on the way of the world with a back thrust of his bauble, which leaves Viola stunned for a short moment:

> VIO. I saw thee late at the Count Orsino's.
> CLOWN. Foolery, sir, does walk about the orb like the sun; it shines everywhere. I would be sorry, sir, but the fool should be as oft with your master as with my mistress. I think I saw your wisdom there. (*Twel.* III, i, 42)

However, the fools of the early Tudor stage were seldom so clever or subtle.

The Marcolf of Birck's *Sapientia Solomonis*, acted before the Queen by the Westminster Boys on 17 January 1565/6, is something of a disappointment as a stage fool. The mythical buffoon had donned motley in at least one German Carnival play of the fifteenth century. But in this Latin play of the mid-sixteenth century, Marcolf has lost all of his wit and retained only his grossness. He is a crude railer against lecherous women. In a parody of Solomon's judgment between the rival claims of two mothers, Marcolf awards the dead child to a harlot, using his customary scurrility (III, iv, 55).[24] But when the outraged woman attacks him, the terrified fool seeks sanctuary with Solomon. Marcolf has not only turned cowardly braggart; he has even become the gull of a pair of rough artisans who scornfully gloat, "we have jeered so openly at this dolt and he doesn't even know it" (V, ii, 54). The transformation from wit to butt, from clever fool to simpleton could hardly be more complete.

Robert Greene introduces a professional jester to Henry III, in his play *The Honorable Historie of frier Bacon and frier Bongay* (c. 1589). But Ralph Simnell is rather a dull fool; his wit is mostly a matter of verbal shifts and chop-logic. His scheme to pose as Prince Edward is no attempt at parody but is imposture pure and simple. And when Friar Bacon, seeing through the fool's disguise, conjures his violent hands, Ralph becomes the butt even of little Miles.

RAPHE. Why, servant Ned, will not the frier doe it? Were not my sword glued to my scabbard by conjuration, I would cut off his head, and make him do it by force.
MILES. In faith, my lord, your manhood and your sword is all alike; they are so fast conjured that we shall never see them. (sc. v, ll. 89–93)

Although he is sometimes regarded as a domestic fool, Slipper, in Greene's *James The Fourth* (c. 1591), is really a clownish servant who is more deceitful and doltish than is Ralph Simnell. Nano the Dwarf, in this play, does show some true flashes of the domestic fool's wit in repartee:

ANDR. Why sot why calst thou me foole?
NANO. For examining wiser then thy selfe.
ANDR. So doth many more then I in *Scotland*.
NANO. Yea those are such, as haue more autthoritie then wit,
And more wealth then honestie. (ll. 437–441)[25]

Greene did little to advance the role of the court fool in Elizabethan drama. He left him about where he had found him, among the jesting Vices of the moral interludes. His Ralph Simnell and Slipper are far more like Common Conditions and Cacurgus and other intriguing impostors than they are like the ironical Touchstone and Feste. But following Greene's plays, the Vice-fool underwent binary fission, one part continuing as rogue and impostor, the other splitting off to become a witty jester and commentator. The rogue developed into the wit-intriguer of

the later Elizabethan and Jacobean Stage. The witty jester and ironical commentator did not re-emerge until the time of Shakespeare and Samuel Rowley, about a decade later.

We need to disregard chronology and go back about a half century to find a stage fool who approaches those of Shakespeare in the quality of his wit and wisdom. He is Gelasimus in Nicholas Grimald's Latin play on the martyrdom of John the Baptist–*Archipropheta* (1547). It would be interesting to assume that Shakespeare knew Grimald's play and went to it for hints for his tragic Fool in *Lear*, but the evidence is all against such a conjecture. A more reasonable assumption is that Shakespeare and Grimald were merely using and transforming a common tradition. Gelasimus scornfully gibes at the Pharisees, speaks some plain home truths to Herodias, and cynically advises John to mask his true thoughts and feelings. By warning John, "you are pursuing a horned beast. If you will listen to me, you will learn to play a part. He cannot live who cannot be cunning" (IV, v, 27), Gelasimus anticipates the Fool who offers shrewd, cynical advice to Kent and the King (*Lear* I, iv, 111; II, iv, 72). And he is no quicker than that later Fool to follow his own mundane advice. Both fools are but echoing the counsel reportedly given to Sir Thomas More's daughter by the fool Patteson: "For the love of safety, then, Mistress Meg, . . . bid thy good father e'en take a fool's advice, and eat humble-pie betimes; for doubt not this proud madame [Anne Boleyn] to be as vindictive as Herodias, and one that, unless he appease her full early, will have his head set before her in a charger. I've said my say."[26] Gelasimus is no innocent unfamiliar with the bitter ways of this world.

Herod's fool gibes at both the lust-dieted Queen and the hypocritical Pharisees in a brief interchange:

SYR. GIRL. My good sir, where have you been?
GELASIMUS. In hell.
SYR. GIRL. In hell? What, pray, did you see there?
GELASIMUS. A devil having his breakfast.
SYR. GIRL. What, pray, did he have for breakfast?
GELASIMUS. Pharisees and women. (IV, v, 3)

At another place, the fool taunts Herodias on her adultery and is promptly rewarded with a box on the ears. His gloomy rejoinder that "truth ever begets hatred, and blows as well! As long as I live I will never again speak the truth" (IV, ii, 32) reminds us of the remarks of Lear's Fool that "Truth's a dog must to kennel; he must be whipp'd out" (*Lear* I, iv, 124). Gelasimus is a bitter fool who lacks the pathetic grace and loyalty of the

Fool in *Lear*, but he is akin to Shakespeare's wise fool in his truth telling and his mocking irony.

With the advent of Touchstone, the witty stage fool came completely into his own, divorced alike from the Vice and the clown. Shakespeare had come to realize, as Chapman and Jonson never did, that the comic spirit breathes most freely in the person of a somewhat detached observer. He had run into the problem with Falstaff, whose comic genius grew too large for the dimensions of a tight little Prodigal Son play. On that occasion, Shakespeare had been forced to follow Procrustes' methods. When he came to rewrite Lodge's *Rosalynde* (1590) for the stage, he was not hampered by history and he found it possible to add the roles of Touchstone and Jaques without seriously disturbing the original plot. The need to keep his wise fool unfettered by the bonds of the plot may have dictated one of the minor inconsistencies in *Twelfth Night*. Maria, it will be remembered, had assigned a part to Feste in the intrigue against Malvolio (II, iii, 188). However, his place is taken in the gulling scene by the relatively colorless Fabian. Why did Shakespeare change his plans for Feste? Could it be that Feste as the wise fool had another, quite different role to play than that of wit-intriguer?

The stage fool plays a less active role in his play than does the comic Vice, but a no less significant part. He retains the Vice's mocking humor and adds some verbal shifts and tricks of his own. He is sometimes a skillful parodist. But the fool as an ironical commentator on the other persons and the action of the play goes far beyond the jesting Vice as a critic. And though he takes no prominent part in the business of the play, he does not merely stand in the wings of the stage and wink at the audience. Try to imagine *As You Like It* without Touchstone or *Twelfth Night* without Feste, and you have some measure of the fool's importance. By his very presence, Shakespeare's wise fool alters the tone and the meaning of the play of which he is a part. The same may not be said of some non-Shakespearean fools whom we are about to consider.

Chapter III. ELIZABETHAN FOOLS and CLOWNS

THE MAN IN MOTLEY enjoyed a rather brief life on the Tudor and Stuart stage. Gelasimus, in Grimald's *Archipropheta* (1547), was probably the first fool in cap-and-bells to appear in the English theatre. By 1626, Gossip Tattle, in Jonson's *The Staple of the News*, reminisces pleasantly of the old days when "there was no Play without a Foole, and a Diuell in't" (ll. 34–35).[1] There is not more than a handful of professional fools in all the plays of this prolific period, and only a few of these deserve the epithet "wise." None of them compare with Shakespeare's fools either in the pungency of their wit or in the warmth of their feelings. Marston gives us two fools, Middleton, one, and Samuel Rowley, one. The two or three Fletcherian fools, who appear in plays after 1616, add nothing to our concept of wise folly or to our understanding of Shakespeare's genius. If we pause to look at some of the lesser fools and clowns of this period, our excuse is that the characters of Touchstone, Feste, and Lear's Fool will stand forth sharply when seen "like bright metal on a sullen ground" (*1 Hen. IV* I, ii, 236).

First among these is Passarello, the fool in Marston's *The Malcontent* (1604), who appears only in those scenes which were inserted when the play was revised for the King's Men. There seems to be little reason to question Marston's authorship of these additions. Certainly Passarello bears a family resemblance to Marston's other fool, Dondolo. That the fool was added suggests that his role is a completely separable and adventitious part of the play's structure. Marston doubtless added the part to satisfy the demands of theatrical expediency. Indications are that *The Malcontent* was originally written for the Children of the Revels. When the play was adapted for the public stages, something had to be supplied to fill the gaps where there had been music in the Blackfriars' performance.[2] Next to music, what could be more entertaining than a little bawdy jesting? Besides, Robert Armin had made the fool's role fashionable in the theatre by 1604.

Passarello, however, has little in common with the wise fools of Shakespeare's plays. He may owe something of his inspiration to Lavache, the least characteristic of Shakespeare's fools, although he is even less amiable.[3] Malevole regards Passarello with the usual attitude of amused contempt:

MAL. *Passarello*, why doe great men begge fooles?

PASS. As the Welchman stole rushes, when there was nothing else to filch; onely to keepe begging in fashion.
MAL. Pue, thou givest no good reason, Thou speakest like a foole. (I, vii, 111)

And for once we are constrained to agree with Malevole. This fool will serve to toy away an idle half hour, and, as Touchstone does for Jaques, he provides Malevole with an excuse to moralize and rail upon the world: "O world most vilde, when thy loose vanities / Taught by this foole, do make the fooles seeme wise!" (I, vii, 145).

But there is a world of difference between Passarello and Touchstone. Passerello is closer in spirit to Jaques or even to Shakespeare's Thersites. He is a railing buffoon in motley. He uses scurrility and salacious wit as only a buffoon can or will. When he uses the label "a natural fool," he is describing not himself but his old master, the court toady Bilioso. In setting forth his relationship to his master, he calls to mind the parasite of Roman drama rather than the wise fool of tradition: "Well Ile dog my Lord, and the word is proper: for when I fawne upon him hee feedes me; when I snap him by the fingers, hee spittes in my mouth" (III, i, 147). Here is a bitter fool indeed, one to whom the epithet is fittingly applied. Yet there seems to be little doubt as to Marston's intentions. His fool, though no very brilliant specimen, is meant to be a mocking jester. But since the stream can be no purer than its source, Passarello is full of turgid and muddy scurrilities. In speaking of the old bawd Maquerelle, he uses appropriately foul language: "Faith I was wont to salute her as our English women are at their first landing in *Flushing*. I would call her whoore; but now that antiquitie leaves her as an old peece of plasticke t' work by, I onely aske hir how her rotten teeth fare every morning, and so leave her . . . she were an excellent Lady, but that hir face peeleth like Muscovie glasse" (I, vii, 123).

Along with the license to speak unpleasant truths and impudently criticize his master, the fool was free to utter uncouth and obscene language. Therefore, Passarello, Will Summers, and Lavache are merely exercising their prerogative as licensed fools when they indulge in coarse and ribald speech. This wanton behavior was carried much further by the zanni of the Italian stage, who acted out their indecencies with lewd language and gestures.[4] Passarello has as much right to joke tiresomely about the horns of cuckoldry as does Touchstone or Lavache. Even such chaste ladies as Rosalind and Beatrice are not above jesting of this crude sort (*A.Y.L.* IV, i, 59; *Much* II, i, 46). However, there is something exceedingly repulsive and humorless about the leering fool who one moment can rail upon the old drab Maquerelle and the next can offer to embrace her "below the loynes" (V, i, 94).

In another passage, Passarello exhibits the same prurient pleasure in lingering over what he satirizes as does his author, John Marston.[5]

BIL. Foole, thou shalt stand for the faire Lady.

PASS. Your foole will stand for your Lady most willingly and most uprightly.

BIL. Ile salute her in Latine.

PASS. O your foole can understand no Latine.

BIL. I but your Lady can.

PASS. Why then if your Lady take downe your foole, your foole will stand no longer for your Lady.

BIL. A pestilent foole: fore God I thinke the world be turnde upside downe too.

PASS. O no sir; for then your Lady and all the Ladies in the pallace should go with their heeles upward, and that were a strange sight you know. (III, i, 120)

This witty innuendo has its own excuse for being, but as satire it is too equivocal to be effective. Like the "rascal beadle" described by Lear (IV, vi, 164), Passarello licks his lips as he whips the back of lechery. The fool by his presence brings nothing to the understanding or enjoyment of *The Malcontent*. For the most part, Passarello but echoes the bitter tirades of Malevole in a minor key. His occasional flashes of wit and his constant flow of scurrilities do nothing to lighten the macabre gloom that hangs ominously over this play.

Marston's other fool, Dondolo in *The Fawne*, was apparently modelled upon the playwright's conception of the "bald fool" of classical tradition. He is closer to the *scurra*, the railing jester and parasite, than to the *sannio*, the grimacing buffoon, and nearer both of these than he is to Shakespeare's wise fool. Although he is quite verbose, Dondolo is occasionally pointed in his satire. He is also more ironical than is Passarello. In answer to Nymphadoro's sarcastic "Art thou growne wise?" and the badgering of the other gallants, Dondolo admits, "I have had a good wit" (I, ii, 30, 42). But in a later scene the fool strikes back at the gossiping court gallants, shielding himself with mock-modesty:

HEROD. Indeed *fatis agimur, cedite fatis*, but how runs rumor what breath's strongest in the Pallace, nowe I thinke you knowe all.

DON. Yes wee fooles thinke wee knowe all . . . (IV, i, 236)

Some of his gibes at foolish philosophers remind us remotely of Lucian's

Sale of Creeds, though the subject of his satire, drawn from antiquity, was hardly relevant to the people in Marston's audience. Dondolo is describing some candidates for a new "Ship of Fools" about to be launched:

HERC. But what Philosophers ha ye.
DON. O very strange fellows one knowes nothing, dares not aver, he lives, goes, sees, feeles.
NYM. A most insensible Philosopher.
DON. An other that there is no present time, and that one man to-day, and to-morrow is not the same man, so that he that yesterday owed money to-day owes none, because he is not the same man.
HERO. Would that Philosopher would hold good in law.
HERC. But why has the Duke thus labord to have all the fools shipt out of his dominions.
DON. Marry because he would play the foole himselfe alone without any rivall. (IV, i, 216)

This show of impudent wit is in keeping with the behavior of the wise fool of court and stage tradition. But as a rule Dondolo merely seconds Hercules in his not too fortunate sallies of wit. In drawing upon the didactic tradition of Lydgate, Brandt, and Barclay, Marston misses the fine ironical touch to be found in the wise fools of Erasmus, Grimald, and Shakespeare. Marston's fools are malicious Vices with their venom drawn.

Middleton, as might be expected, gives us a bawdy, tipsy fool in Pickadill of *No Wit, No Help Like a Woman's* (? 1613). Pickadill shows as strong a taste for scabrous jesting as Passarello does. And yet there is a subtle difference between their brands of bawdry. We have already noted the prurient element in the jesting of Passarello—and Marston. Middleton, however, seems to be completely free of moral or satirical intentions, and his fool is franker, wittier, and more ironical in his comments than are Passarello and Dondolo. Pickadill's chief butt is the pseudo-learned Weatherwise, who carries his almanac about with him. In mocking the astrologer, he uses a sexual metaphor almost Falstaffian in quality:

WEA. So, set the table ready; the widow's i' the next room, looking upon my clock with the days and the months and the change of the moon; I'll fetch her in presently. (*Exit.*
PICK. She's not so mad to be fetched in with the moon, I warrant you: a man must go roundlier to work with a widow, than to woo her with the hand of a dial, or stir up her blood with the striking part of a clock; I should ne'er stand to show her such things in chamber. (II, i, 1)[6]

The convention that the professional fool is a little slow or short of wits is maintained here as in most plays containing fools. Weatherwise hails Pickadill, "Mass, here's her ladyship's ass; he tells us anything" (III, i, 84). But after some very strained jesting about a sun-cup that has passed through the twelve signs of the zodiac, Weatherwise appreciatively comments, "The fool will live, madame." To which statement Pickadill sardonically replies, "Ay, as long as your eyes are open, I warrant him" (II, i, 315). Elsewhere, he plays ambiguously with the term "fool":

WEA. This quarrel must be drowned.—Pickadill, my lady's fool.
PICK. Your, your own man, sir. (II, i, 213)

My Lady Goldenfleece's fool reminds us of the old Countess of Rossillion's fool in *All's Well that Ends Well.* Both are witty, urbane, and sensual, and both enjoy puncturing the pretentions of a mock gallant. But Pickadill exhibits nowhere that true gallantry and tenderness which Lavache shows toward the Lady Helena. Although he is a clever artificial fool, Pickadill lacks that wisdom which transcends shrewdness, that gayety which is beyond buffoonery. We can hardly expect to find such combination of qualities in any jester outside the plays of Shakespeare.

Of the non-Shakespearean fools which we are here considering, Will Summers in Samuel Rowley's chronicle play *When You See Me, You Know Me* (1603–1605) is by far the most interesting. Rowley follows the hearsay of history in bringing to the stage this popular jester. Henry VIII, who had more fools than wives, seems to have been especially fond of Will. The King is reported to have accepted the fool's counsel even in matters of state. An anecdote related by Robert Greene illustrates Will's proverbial shrewdness. Asked by the King to decide between three claimants for a strip of land, two courtiers, represented by attorneys, and the Yeoman of the Pantry, the fool replied in the following fashion. Taking out a walnut and cracking it neatly in half, Will handed one empty half-shell to one lawyer, the other half-shell to the other lawyer, and the meat of the nut to his friend the Yeoman. With a calculated slur at the pettifoggers, he remarked: "so shal thy gift be *Harry* . . ., this lawyer shal haue good Bookes, and this, faire promises, but my felow of the Pantry shal haue the land. For thus deale they with their clyents."[7]

Robert Armin, the kindly jester of Shakespeare's company, is authority for a sympathetic, if not wholly reliable account of the actual Will Summers:

> In he [Summers] comes, and finding the king at dinner and the cardinall by attending, to disgrace him that he neuer loved,

> Harry, sayes hee, lend me ten pound. What to doe? saies the king. To pay three or foure of the cardinall's creditors, quoth hee, to whom my word is past, and they come now for the money. That thou shalt, Will, quoth hee. Creditors of mine? saies the cardinall: Ile give your grace my head if any man can justly aske me a penny. No! saies Will. Lend me ten pounds; if I pay it not where thou owest it, Ile give thee twenty for it. Doe so, saies the king. That I will, my liege, saies the cardinall, though I know I owe none. With that he lends Will ten pounds. Will goes to the gate, distributes it to the poore, and brought the empty bag. There is thy bag againe, saies hee: thy creditors are satisfied, and my word out of danger.
>
> Who received? sayes the king; the brewer or the baker? Neyther (Harry), saies Will Sommers. But, Cardinall, answere me one thing: to who dost thou owe thy soule? To God, quoth hee. To whom thy wealth? To the poore, sayes hee. Take thy forfeit (Harry) sayes the foole; open confession, open penance: his head is thine, for to the poore at the gate I paid his debt, which he yeelds is due. . . . The king laught at the jest, and so did the cardinall for a shew, but it grieved him to jest away ten pounds so. . . .[8]

Rowley's characterization of Will Summers, based in part upon Armin's account, is fully in the tradition of the wise fool. His Summers is a little shrewder and less kindly than was his prototype.[9] He shows himself discreet to the point of cowardice in one scene with the Cardinal's natural fool Patch. When Will is asked to jest the King out of a black mood, he sends poor Patch in before him to take off the edge of the King's displeasure:

WILL. I'll stand behind the post here, and thou shalt go softly stealing behind him as he sits reading yonder, and when thou comest close to him, cry Bo! and we'll scare him so, he shall not tell where to rest him.

PATCH. But will he not be angry?

WILL. No, no, for then I'll show myself, and after he sees who 'tis, he'll laugh and be as merry as a mag-pie, and thou'lt be made man by it, for all the house shall see him hug thee in his arms and dandle thee up and down with hand and foot as thou wert a football.

PATCH. O fine! Come, cousin, give me the point first and I'll roar so loud, that I'll make him believe, that the devil's come. (Elze ed., p. 21)

Will Summers deserves censure when he treats the simple Patch to the same scornful laughter that is flung at him and his fellow fools.

The passage just quoted aptly illustrates the difference between natural and artificial fools—a difference which Armin defines in a bit of doggerel verse: "Naturall fooles are prone to selfe conceipt: / Fooles artificiall, with their wits lay wayte / To make themselues fooles, liking the disguise, / To feede their owne mindes, and the gazers eyes" (Armin, p. 12). Will Summers, like most artificial fools, is perfectly willing to be taken for a simple fool. Near the beginning of the play, he arrives on the scene, booted and spurred, blowing a horn. His appearance amuses the King, and some verbal sparring follows:

KING. How now, William? What, post post? Where have you been riding?
WILL. Out of my way, Old Harry. I am all on the spur, I can tell ye, I have tidings worth telling.
KING. Why, where hast thou been?
WILL. Marry, I rise early and ride post to London, to know what news was here at court.
KING. Was that your nearest way, William?
WILL. O, ay, the very foot-path; but yet I rid the horseway to hear it. I warrant there is ne'er a conduit-head keeper in London, but knows what is done in all the courts of christendom.

At this point the Cardinal joins the game and asks:

WOL. And what is the best news there, William?
WILL. Good news for you, my lord cardinal, for one of the old women waterbearers told me for certain, that last Friday all the bells in Rome rang backward: there was a thousand dirges sung, six hundred Ave-maries said, every man washed his face in holy water, the people crossing and blessing themselves to send them a new pope, for the old is gone to Purgatory.

When Wolsey bursts out laughing, Summers drops his mask of foolishness and turns on him derisively: "Nay, my lord, you'ld laugh if it were so, indeed, for every body thinks, if the pope were dead, you gape for a benefice . . ." (pp. 7–8).

With the King and the Cardinal, Will Summers is brazenly familiar, but at least once when he is alone with Patch he puts on an assumed modesty. To Patch's invitation to spend the night in the Cardinal's wine-cellar, Will replies: "We have but a little wit between us already cousin, and so we should have none at all" (p. 40). But Will's pretense to witlessness deceives no one, nor is it meant to. The other characters all bear witness to Summers' cleverness. "What a knavish fool's this" (p. 24), observes the King. "A shrewd fool" (p. 38), admits Wolsey with grudging admiration. "The fool tells true" (pp. 12, 41) and "He is too hard for me" (pp. 39, 77 f.) echo like refrains throughout the play. Will has no mean opinion of his own intelligence as his tart rejoinders show. Often his witticisms play upon the several meanings of the word "fool." For example, when Wolsey greets him with "How now, William? What, are you here too?" Summers maliciously replies, "Ay, my lord, all the fools follow you" (p. 17). In another passage, reminiscent of the scene between Olivia and Feste in *Twelfth Night* (I, v, 41), Henry gives the order, "Take hence the fool." To this command, Will saucily answers: "Ay, when? can ye tell? Dost thou think any o'th lords will take the fool? None here, I warrant, except the cardinal" (p. 24). Will also has his jest at the expense of such pedantic clergymen as Archbishop Cranmer when Prince Ned orders the fool thrust out of his presence: "Well, *cedant arma togae*, the scholars shall have the fool's place" (p. 51).

The trait which Rowley most emphasizes in Will is his blunt truth-telling. More than once the King comments that "the fool tells true." And when Wolsey objects, "You speak plain, William," Summers retorts, "Ye never knew fool a flatterer, I warrant ye" (p. 39). He will speak the truth and shame the Cardinal. His humor may be too bawdy and his wisdom too sectarian, but there is no denying his keen wit. Using the simple Patch as a whetstone, he turns the sharp edge of his scorn upon Wolsey and wounds him with a glancing stroke:

WOL. You are too crafty for him [Patch], William.
KING. So is he, Wolsey, credit me.
WILL. I think so, my lord: as long as Will lives, the cardinal's fool must give way to the king's fool. (p. 23)

Will Summers is indeed a truth speaker and satirical commentator. However, his barbed comments might easily have flown by like bird-bolts, stinging but not seriously bruising his targets. Evidently Rowley intended that Will should fulfill a more active role in the play than that of ironical bystander. He is made the chief intriguer against Wolsey. Through his means the Cardinal is exposed in all his cupidity and cruel avarice. This use of the fool as wit-intriguer and plot manipulator recalls the role assigned the jesting Vice in the Tudor interlude. But the fool is no Vice in Rowley's scheme of things. He is no misleader of the King, nor is he opposed to the good as the Vice must be. Nevertheless, the dramatic importance attached to Will Summers in *When You See Me, You Know Me* stretches the fool out of character and destroys his comic detachment.

However witty or consciously ironical they may be, the fools that we have considered thus far have a certain brittle, callous quality about them.

They are witty fools but scarcely wise in the Erasmian sense. They are without that human warmth and fellow feeling that characterizes even the least attractive of Shakespeare's fools. Indeed, we must look outside the narrow ring of professional fools to find characters as genial as Touchstone, as gay as Feste, or as loyal as Lear's Fool. Three domestic clowns who double as household servants, and are therefore not fools in the strict sense of the word, deserve our attention. The clown Robin in Wilkins' *The Miseries of Enforced Marriage* (1607), Shadow in Dekker's *Old Fortunatus* (1599), and Babulo in Haughton, Chettle, and Dekker's *The Pleasant Comodie of Patient Grissill* (1600) resemble Shakespeare's fools in their kindliness and in their loyal devotion to their master or mistresses. But before considering these jester-like clowns, we need to distinguish clearly between the fool and the clown of stage tradition. It is interesting to note that Robin, the clown, and Feste, the jester, are consistently addressed as "fool" throughout the plays in which they appear, and both are designated "clown" in the tags before their speeches. The stage practice of loosely labelling all low comedy figures "clowns" has tended to obscure for us the very real difference between the fool and the clown—a distinction which was clearly understood by the people of Shakespeare's day. Whatever their labels, Passarello, Dondolo, Pickadill, and Will Summers were obviously meant to be fools by profession.

Originally, of course, the clown was a clumsy country bumpkin. On the stage he was differentiated from his fellows by his coarse, provincial idiom, a species of rustic dialect sometimes called "Cotswold speech." The clown was usually dressed differently from the stage fool. In his vitriolic tirade against plays and players, the puritan William Rankins marks the two apart by their clothing: ". . . some trans-formed themselues to Roges, other to Ruffians, some other to Clownes, a fourth to fooles. . . . The Roges were ready, the Ruffians were rude, theyr Clownes cladde as well with Country Condition, as in Ruffe russet, theyr Fooles as fonde as might be . . ."[10] Although the actual court fool may not have worn motley and bells except on state occasions, the stage jester wore this garb to distinguish him from other players. There is another, more important way in which the fool and the stage clown differ. They vary in the kind and quality of the humor which they employ. Sometimes, like Hodge in *Gammer Gurtons Nedle* (c. 1553), the clown is a dull clod without a glimmer of brightness or quickness about him. Or like People, a character in the Catholic morality *Respublica* (1553), he is boorish in speech and manners yet not without a streak of salty good sense. But the English clown is often a creature of contradictions. Like the stage buffoon of classical and Cinquecento comedy, he is alternately clever and stupid, the wit and the butt, in the comic business of the play. Shakespeare's Launce comes close to being the archetype for this kind of humor.

Finally, the fool and the clown differ in the relative importance each is given in the play's structure. The fool is usually detached from the main action, but he is not irrelevant to the theme of the play. That Shakespeare could add Touchstone, Feste, Lavache and Lear's Fool to the old plays or stories upon which his dramas were based is proof of the fool's relative detachment. That he did add them immeasurably enhances the meaning and the beauty of these plays. There is some evidence that the clown's role had come to be regarded as an impertinent excrescence on the dramatic action. All Shakespearean students will remember Hamlet's advice to the players wherein he particularly cautions the clown against improvising his lines and usurping more than belongs to his part (*Ham.* III, ii, 42). That the clown's jigs and buffoonery were often independent turns with no bearing on the rest of the play was made the subject of ridicule in the Cambridge comedy *The Pilgrimage to Parnassus* (c. 1598). When a clown is protestingly drawn on the stage with a cart rope, he is told that "Clownes haue bene thrust into playes by head & shoulders, euer since Kempe could make a scuruey face" (ll. 665–667).[11] The fools in the plays of Shakespeare and his contemporaries are characters in the plot, not irrelevant entertainers who wander across the stage at will. They are more consciously ironical in their humor than are the clowns. This trait could easily degenerate into a self-conscious affectation, and it sometimes does in the fools of Marston and Middleton. Shakespeare, as we shall see, levied on the best resources of both traditions in compounding his wise fools.

Returning to an examination of the jester-like clowns, Robin, Shadow, and Babulo, we immediately notice how much more closely they resemble Shakespeare's fools than they do the clowns of stage tradition. The only thing that disqualifies them as professional fools is that they are tied to the plots of their plays as comic servants. Robin is identified as a servant by his blue coat, the livery of a domestic:

> ILF. But stay, here is a Scrape-trencher arriued:
> How now blew bottle, are you of the house?[12]

But he serves only as a messenger in the play, a function which Touchstone, Feste, and Lavache all perform. Robin certainly links himself with members of the merry profession when he enters singing, "From London am I come, tho not with pipe and drum . . ." (sig. C3ᵛ.). There is an old print (Harleian MS. 3885, f. 19) which represents Tarlton with pipe and tabor. And of course, Feste enters at the beginning of Act III of *Twelfth Night* with tabor and pipe. If Fleay is correct in asserting that Armin played the role of Robin,[13] the famous actor of fools may have infused something of the spirit of Feste into the part.

Although Robin does not play a very long or prominent part in Wilkins' tragedy, we see enough of him to wish that he might come on the scene more often. He is almost the only bright or attractive figure in an otherwise dreary melodrama. His wits are never held in question; yet the clown insists upon his wisdom in contrast to the folly of others.

WENTLOE. Sblud this is a philosophicall foole.
CLOWN. Then I that am a foole by Art, am better then you that are fooles by nature. (sig. A2v.)

This is the familiar paradox which ironical fools have delighted in since the time of Marcolf. It was a favorite trick of humanists like Erasmus to juxtapose wisdom and folly in such a way as to reverse their ordinary meanings. Armin, who had a taste for such things, may have been responsible for inserting this proverbial bit of fool's wisdom in the play.

Whether or not Wilkins ever collaborated with Shakespeare, the writer of *The Miseries of Enforced Marriage* was probably indebted to the great comic poet for his conception of a gentle, whimsical fool. A passage of pedantic quibbling, of which all professional fools are fond, unmistakably echoes Feste's pleasantries and the Fool's censuring of Lear:

ILF. Well Sir, are you of the house?
CLOW. No Sir, I am twenty yardes without, and the house stands without me.
BART. Prethee tels who owes this building.
CLOW. He that dwels in it Sir.
ILF. Who dwels in it then.
CLOW. He that owes it.
ILF. Whats his name.
CLOW. I was none of his God-father.
ILF. Dos maister Scarberow lie heere,
CLOW. Ile giue you a rime for that Sir,
Sicke men may lie, and dead men in their Graues,
Few else do lie abed at noone, but Drunkards, Punks, & knaues.
ILF. What am I the better for thy answer?
CLOW. What am I the better for thy question?
ILF. Why nothing.
CLOW. Why then of nothing comes nothing. (sigs. A2, A2v.)

Robin also reminds us of Lear's Fool in his devotion to his mistress. Like the tender-hearted creature who "hath much pined away" (*Lear* I, iv, 80) since Cordelia's banishment to France, Robin commiserates his mistress Clare, whose husband has forsaken her. And yet at the same time he manages to mock his own sorrow in hyperbolic terms: "O mistris, if euer you haue seene *Demoniceacleare* look into mine eyes, mine eyes are *Seuerne*, plaine *Seuerne*, the Thames, nor the Ryuer of *Tweed* are nothing to em: Nay all the rayne that fell at *Noahs* floud, had not the discretion that my eyes haue: that drunke but vp the whole world, and I ha drown all the way betwixt this and London" (sig. C3v.). We take our leave of Robin early in the second act but not before the clown has stamped his impress upon our minds.

Shadow, the clownish servant in Dekker's *Old Fortunatus*, has some traits in common with Babulo and Shakespeare's fools. Like Feste, he dissembles his true nature but regrets "that a false face should become any man" (IV, ii, 100).[14] He shows awareness of the fool's paradox when he humbly remarks, "I feare nothing, but that whilst wee striue to make others fooles, we shall weare the Coxcombes our selues" (IV, ii, 107). In much the same manner that Lear's Fool berates his King, Shadow uses the fool's license to reprove his master Andelocia for his prodigality: "Its happie I haue a leane wit: but master, you haue none; for when your money tript away, that went after it, and euer since you haue beene mad" (II, ii, 14). Again he reminds us of Babulo and Lear's Fool in his stubborn loyalty that goes beyond the normal call of duty: "Ile goe hence, because you send me; but ile goe weeping hence, for griefe that I must turne villaine as many doe, and leaue you when you are vp to the eares in aduersitie" (III, i, 495). There is no hint or suggestion that Shadow actually wears motley or that he plays the role of a professional jester, but he is a jester-like clown who is devoted to his young master.

The third of these, Babulo in *Patient Grissill*, is a clown only in the technical sense since he earns his livelihood at basket-weaving– a better trade than that of courtier, as he candidly tells the Marquesse.[15] But we are left in some doubt as to his career at court. There is more than a suggestion that Babulo is to become a jester to the Marquesse:

MARQ. *Grissill* I take delight to heare him talke.

BAB. I, I, y'oare best take me vp for your foole: are not you he, that came speaking so, to *Grissill* heere? doe you remember how I knockt you once for offering to haue a licke at her lips.

MARQ. I doe remember it and for thy paines, A golden recompence ile giue to thee.

BAB. Why doe, and ile knock you as often as you list.
MARQ. *Grissill* this merrie fellow shall be mine . . . (I, ii, 325)

However, his speech upon his dismissal from court does not seem to bear out this supposition: "great was the wisedome of the Taylor, that sticht me in Motley, for hee's a foole that leaues basket making to turne Courtier: I see my destiny dogs me: at first I was a foole (for I was borne an Innocent) then I was a traueller, and then Basket-maker, and then a Courtier, and now I must turne basket-maker and foole againe, the one I am sworne to, but the foole I bestowe vpon the world, for *Stultorum plena sunt omnia* . . ." (III, i, 112). Yet from this and an earlier passage (I, ii, 304) we are told that Babulo wears the traditional garb of a jester.

Why then did not Dekker and his collaborators cast Babulo in the role of professional fool? The answer should be obvious. Old Janiculo could not well have afforded to keep a household jester solely for his amusement. Nor could Babulo have fulfilled his proper function in the play as jester to the Marquesse. This clown is too important dramatically to be restricted to the court and to the few scenes of the underplot. Since the play chiefly concerns the fortunes of Grissill and her family, Babulo must be attached to Janiculo as a servant or apprentice. The case of Babulo apparently contradicts what we have just said about the clown and his dramatic irrelevance. But Babulo is no ordinary clown. His part is as closely integrated with the main action as is that of Feste or Lear's Fool. He is far more necessary to the development of the plot than is Passarello or Pickadill. In his relationship to Laureo, to Grissill, and to the Marquesse, he shows himself most like Shakespeare's wise fools. His ready wit, kindliness, and essential sanity make of Babulo something more than a merely clever clown. When he describes himself ironically: "at first I was a foole (for I was borne an Innocent)," he is, of course, punning on the word. But like the ironical man of antiquity, he pretends to ignorance or stupidity for his own amusement. This is the way that he greets Laureo, newly come home from the university:

BAB. Master *Laureo* (Ianiculaes sonne) welcome home, how doe the nine muses, Pride, couetousnes, enuie, sloth, wrath, gluttonie and letcherie? you that are Schollers read how they doe.
LAUR. Muses: these (foole) are the seauen deadly sins.
BAB. Are they: Mas, me thinkes its better seruing them, then your nine muses, for they are starke beggers. (I, ii, 117)

Like Gelasimus and Lear's Fool, Babulo is quite ready to give cynical advice which he has no intention of following himself.

Babulo, however, reveals his true sanity when he is contrasted with the morose scholar Laureo. Sometimes he laughs good-humoredly at Laureo's ill-natured grumbling:

BAB. Goe *Grissill* Ile make fire, and scoure the kettle, its a hard world when schollers eate fish vpon flesh daies. (I, ii, 158)

. . . .

LAUR. Let's fret and curse the *Marquesse* cruelly.
BAB. I by my troth that's a good way, we may well do it, now we are out of his hearing. (IV, ii, 128)

At another time he loses patience with the disgruntled scholar and speaks bluntly:

BAB. Come I haue left my worke to see what mattens you mumble to your selfe, faith *Laureo* I would you could leaue this lattin, and fal to make baskets, you think tis enough if at dinner you tell vs a tale of Pignies, and then mounch vp our victuals, but that fits not vs: or the historie of the well *Helicon*, and then drinke vp our beare: we cannot liue vpon it.
LAUR. A Scholler doth disdaine to spend his spirits Vpon such base imploiments as hand labours.
BAB. Then you should disdaine to eate vs out of house and home. (V, i, 1)

Most of the time Babulo's unfailing cheerfulness in adversity is set in marked contrast to Laureo's sour discontent.

The clown's sturdy rural ways are opposed to the silken customs of the court. He seems to prefer the rigors of the country to the ease and elegance of the town. When the Marquesse would try Grissill's humility as well as her patience, Babulo's reply is characteristic:

MARQ. I hung this russet gowne,
And this poore pitcher for a monument,
Amongst my costliest Iemmes: see heere they hang,
Grissill looke heere, this gowne is vnlike to this?
GRIS. My gratious Lord, I know full well it is.
BAB. *Grissill* was as pretty a *Grissill* in the one as in the other.
MARQ. You haue forgot these rags, this water pot.
GRIS. With reuerence of your Highnes I haue not.
BAB. Nor I, many a good messe of water grewell has that yeelded vs. (III, i, 81)

In his fondness for water gruel and russet clothes, Babulo shows himself a true born English clown. He would have agreed with the Plowman in

Of Gentylnes and Nobylyte (c. 1522) "To haue fode and cloth and a mery mynde / And to desyre no more than is nedefull- / That is in this worlde the lyf most joyfull . . ."[16] Babulo is a hearty fellow who takes joy in his work and in the drubbing he has given the Marquesse. Feste is probably too old and Lear's Fool too frail for such vigorous living.

Babulo the clown shows his near kinship to Shakespeare's fools in his loyal-hearted devotion to old Janiculo and to his long suffering mistress Grissill. When, near the close of the play, the old man and his family trudge on the scene burdened down with wood and coal, Babulo protests, "Master goe you but vnder the Cole-staffe, *Babulo* can beare all, staffe, basket and all" (V, ii, 52). Earlier his anger has been aroused by the harsh treatment of Grissill and her aged father, and he savagely rails upon Furio: "Th'art a Iewe, th'art a Pagan: howe darst thou leaue them without a cloke for the raine, when his daughter, and his sister, and my Mistris is the Kings wife?" But Babulo soon recovers his sense of humor and remarks, "There's a ship of fooles ready to hoyst sayle, they stay but for a good winde and your company: ha ha ha, I wonder (if all fooles were banisht) where thou wouldst take shipping" (III, i, 28). He reveals his true humanity again when he comes in dandling one of Grissill's babies: "A fig for care, olde Master, but now olde graundsire, take this little Pope Innocent, wee'll giue ouer basket making and turne nurses, shee has vnckled *Laureo*: Its no matter, you shall goe make a fire, Grandsire you shall dandle them, *Grissill* shall goe make Pap, and Ile licke the skillet, but first Ile fetch a cradle . . ." (IV, ii, 40). In his love of children, this gentle clown matches Yorick who bore the boy Hamlet about on his shoulders. And he is more successful than Lear's Fool in his attempt to outjest the "heart-struck injuries" (*Lear* III, i, 17) of his master and mistress. Babulo indeed comes close in spirit to the wise fools of Shakespeare.

Chapter IV. SHAKESPEARE'S WISE FOOLS

Touchstone in Arcadia

"THOU SPEAK'ST WISER than thou art ware of" (*A.Y.L.* II., iv, 57), comments Rosalind of Touchstone, and the fool feeds the complacent superiority of the noble lady by agreeing with her. Jaques, in commending Touchstone to the Duke, gloats over his discovery, "He's as good at anything, and yet a fool" (V, iv, 109). This is as far as Jaques may go in magnanimity. Earlier in the play, Rosalind hails the jester as "Nature's natural the cutter-off of Nature's wit" (I, ii, 52). And Celia welcomes him with even less grace, for, says she, "always the dulness of the fool is the whetstone of the wits" (I, ii, 58). Except for the Duke, whose penetrating comments on the witty fool are well known, the noble characters in the play seem to regard Touchstone as a natural or dull fool who sometimes serves to sharpen the wits of his betters. Certain otherwise astute critics seem to have been misled by these comments upon the fool. Tolman finds that Shakespeare's treatment of Touchstone's character is "somewhat wavering and uncertain."[1] Furness notes an inconsistency between the "simpleton" of the First Act and the wise, satirical fool of Act Five. "Are there not here two separate characters?" he asks.[2]

As for any real or apparent inconsistencies in Touchstone's characterization, they may be explained by reference to certain facts of stage history. If Shakespeare had Will Kempe in mind for the part when he began to write *As You Like It*, he undoubtedly altered the role in some important respects to fit the temper of Robert Armin, the new clown who joined the Chamberlain's Men sometime in 1600.[3] Kempe had acted the roles of such louts as Dogberry and Peter, whereas Armin shows himself a connoisseur of court fools in his book *Foole upon Foole, or Six Sortes of Sottes* (1600). There is another explanation for any discrepancy between the "roynish clown" of Act I and the clever jester of the remainder of the play. It may be that Touchstone disguises his wits when at Frederick's court out of prudent regard for the usurper's authority. Recent bitter experience has taught us over again that tyrants always regard intelligence with suspicion. This theory would also explain Touchstone's freer and happier tongue when he has escaped to the forest.

The attitude of genial condescension which Rosalind and others express was implicit in the relationship of master to fool from the beginning. Fools served a double function: to entertain their masters and mistresses and at the same time to minister to their sense of self-importance. Frequently the fool criticized his lord but always from behind a cloak of assumed inferiority. Such were the hierarchical arrangements of medieval and renaissance society. But a mixture of amusement, contempt, and, sometimes, awe often characterized the popular feelings toward the allowed fool. This peculiar and paradoxical status was the price he had to pay for his relative freedom and license to criticize. The wise fool willingly paid the price and enjoyed the paradox. That he not only accepts his role but even revels in it marks Touchstone off from some less wise fools. Rowley's Will Summers, for example, is almost childishly vain of his shrewd wits. He is enormously pleased with himself when he sacrifices Patch to the King's displeasure and thereby saves himself from a beating. Touchstone apparently acquiesces when Jaques introduces him to the Duke as "the motley-minded gentleman" (V, iv, 41), whereas Feste in jesting with Olivia insists: "I wear not motley in my brain" (*Twel.* I, v, 63). Touchstone never pushes his point or insists unduly on his own good sense. After Rosalind has berated him as a dull fool and has sharpened her metaphorical wit upon him, Touchstone answers simply, "You have said; but whether wisely or no, let the forest judge" (III, ii, 129).

Touchstone exercises his wit through parody, and parody is, of course, the sworn enemy of the didactic. The Duke may read his pretty sermons in stones and running brooks, Jaques may moralize upon the stricken deer, and Orlando pin his lovesick poems to every tree, but the fool looks on and laughingly mimics them. He even triumphs over the robust wit of Rosalind by his burlesque wooing and wedding of Audrey. Like the wise fool that he is, Touchstone alters his manner to fit the quality and the mood of the persons on whom he jests. With his mistress and Rosalind, he is properly subservient except for the occasional impertinence that breaks through. His gross parody of Orlando's lyrics is amusing and apt for the most part. But one can hardly blame a lady for resenting a poem which likens her to a hind or a cat in heat or to a whore carted through the streets of London (III, ii, 114).[4] However, Touchstone's sallies are usually less crude and direct, and they are further softened by a touch of self-mockery. Silvius' recital of his unrequited love for Phebe arouses differing responses in Rosalind and in Touchstone:

ROS. Jove, Jove! this shepherd's passion
Is much upon my fashion.
TOUCH. And mine, but it grows something stale with me. (II, iv, 61)

The gentleman in motley pretends to being on terms of equality with Jaques. Whenever the two meet, Touchstone observes the elaborate punctilios of courtesy between Elizabethan gentlemen, with just a hint of patronizing Jaques who has condescended to him: "Good even, good Master What-ye-call't. How do you, sir? You are very well met. Goddild you for your last company. I am very glad to see you. Even a toy in hand here, sir. Nay, pray be cover'd" (III, iii, 74). Dr. Thümmel, in contrasting Touchstone with Feste, finds that the earlier fool is something of a parvenu courtier and that his courtesy is an affectation.[5] This seems to be a misreading of Touchstone's intentions, for he is obviously parodying courtly manners here just as he later makes fun of the etiquette of the duello[6]. To the Duke, who justly appreciates his intelligence, Touchstone is properly deferential and courteous. There is the accent of genuine humility in his reply to the Duke's praise:

DUKE. S. By my faith, he is very swift and sententious.
TOUCH. According to the fool's bolt, sir, and such dulcet diseases. (V, iv, 65)

By recalling the old proverb, "a fool's bolt is soon shot," he shows that he takes himself no more seriously than he ought to.

But when he encounters the shepherds and rustics, Touchstone adopts a tone as patronizing as Jaques and the ladies take toward him. Corin must smart a little under the fool's assumed superiority:

COR. You have too courtly a wit for me. I'll rest.
TOUCH. Wilt thou rest damn'd? God help thee, shallow man! God make incision in thee, thou art raw! (III, ii, 72)

In saluting the clown William, he is a trifle more condescending than in his manner of greeting Jaques:

TOUCH. Good ev'n, gentle friend. Cover thy head, cover thy head. Nay, prithee be cover'd. How old are you, friend?
WILL. Five-and-twenty, sir.
TOUCH. A ripe age. Is thy name William?
WILL. William, sir.
TOUCH. A fair name. Wast born i' th' forest here?
WILL. Ay, sir, I thank God.
TOUCH. 'Thank God.' A good answer. (V, i, 18)

Suddenly abandoning his friendly tone toward the lout, Touchstone bursts forth with a torrent of turgid and unprovoked abuse: "I will deal in poison with thee, or in bastinado, or in steel. I will bandy with thee in faction; I will o'errun thee with policy; I will kill thee a hundred and fifty ways. Therefore tremble and depart" (V, i, 60). His bluster, of course, is not serious, and the storm dies as quickly as it arises. The furious fustian is not so much directed at poor William, who happens to lie in its path, as it is at poetasters like Marston who use this sort of bombast in all seriousness.[7]

While Touchstone's wit takes the form of parody, his temper is essentially realistic. He is the Vekke keeping watch in the Garden of the Rose, or Pandarus serving at the Court of Love. An even closer analogy to Touchstone in the Forest of Arden would be the garrulous nurse in *Romeo and Juliet*. Like the nurse and like Pandarus, Touchstone acts as a sort of comic catalyst in the golden world. Arden, however, is no less golden for Touchstone's presence there; on the contrary, it becomes infinitely more desirable and more comfortable than the gilt and tinsel world of conventional pastoral. With Touchstone one may sit down in Arden and scratch one's back or rub one's tired feet:

ROS. O Jupiter, how weary are my spirits!
TOUCH. I care not for my spirits, if my legs were not weary. (II, iv, 1)

Touchstone is the critic inside the play. As C. S. Lewis has observed of the medieval dream-allegory: "Above all it protects itself against the laughter of the vulgar—that is, of all of us in certain moods—by allowing laughter and cynicism their place *inside* the poem. . . . In the same way, the comic figures in a medieval love poem are a cautionary concession—a libation made to the god of lewd laughter. . ."[8] Touchstone's presence within the pastoral romance is a concession to our sense of comic realism and protects the play from corrosive criticism.

Realism surely borders on the grotesque in Touchstone's wooing of Audrey. What romantic lover—what lover, for that matter—would exclaim over his loved one, "Well, praised be the gods for thy foulness! Sluttishness may come hereafter" (III, iii, 40)? Who would allude to his bride-to-be as "A poor virgin, sir, an ill-favour'd thing, sir, but mine own" (V, iv, 60)? Who, but Touchstone? And the court fool comes pressing in "amongst the rest of the country copulatives, to swear and to forswear, according as marriage binds and blood breaks" (V, iv, 57). Do these speeches of the fool show him to be a cynic, disillusioned with love and the dream of fair ladies? Hardly! Touchstone is a genial humorist, not a caustic critic.[9] True, he laughs good-naturedly at the silly extravagances and conventions of pastoral love, but at the same time he shows a wholesome regard for the realities of marriage: "As the ox has his bow, sir, the horse his curb and the falcon her bells, so man hath his desires; and as pigeons bill, so wedlock would be nibbling" (III, iii, 80). Nature must have her due. And who knows this truth better than the court fool turned rustic philosopher?

Whether we regard Touchstone as a grotesque philosopher or as the realistic *punctum indifferens* of the play, we must grant his wisdom. John Palmer has neatly summed up the quality of the fool's wisdom in a sentence: "He will see things as they are but without malice."[10] However, Mr. Palmer's statement needs a slight emendation so that it will read: "He will see things as they are *in nature* but without malice." For Touchstone is a natural philosopher and realist. He is witty and penetrating enough to see physical love behind the illusory mask of the pastoral lovers and to note the peevishness and self-pity behind Jaques' affected melancholy. Although he ironically joins the merry dance to the altar at the end of the play, Touchstone is too hardheaded to live happily in the forest of romance. This wise fool is a critic, and the astringency of his wit is both his strongest asset and his chief liability. His mocking humor enables us to laugh at pretense and vulgar folly, but it cannot open our eyes to the true if transitory loveliness of the Arcadian dream. This unearthly charm is beyond the ken of the witty but worldly fool. While it is true that Shakespeare's conception of the wise fool grew and reached a finer flowering in the later plays, it is equally true that Touchstone is a wise and thoroughly witty fool.

The Artful Feste

The same actor who played Touchstone undoubtedly acted the roles of Feste, Lavache, and Lear's Fool. And since Shakespeare must have written the parts with Robert Armin in mind, we may expect to find a family likeness in them all. Touchstone and Feste do have a great deal in common. They appear in the brightest and best comedies, written in Shakespeare's happiest vein probably within a year of each other. Both fools are in a sense the moving spirits of the plays in which they appear. Needless to say, they are both perfectly sane. They are witty and wise and ironical fools. However, the differences between the two are as noteworthy as their similarities. Some of the difference between Touchstone and Feste lies in the roles assigned them in the plays. Feste is a singer and charms us with his music as much as with his wit. Amiens sings the lyrics in *As You Like It;* whereas Touchstone merely chatters some doggerel. Feste's singing of "O mistress mine" and the lovely song at the close of the play makes him especially attractive and probably swings the balance in his favor. But if we like him chiefly for his songs, we are judging him as an entertainer, not necessarily as a wise fool. Because he is a minstrel at home in Illyria, Feste must act in a slightly different way from Touchstone in the Forest of Arden. Touchstone parodies and pokes good-natured fun at the romantic extravagances of Arcadia. Feste upholds the old order, the *status quo ante* in Illyria—and in England. Mark Van Doren happily hits the tonic key of *Twelfth Night* when he calls it a drama between the mind of Malvolio and "the music of old manners."[11] That phrase might serve as a fairly accurate description of the role that Feste plays.

Of course, no one in the play really doubts the fool's wits. Olivia does term him "a dry fool" (*Twel.* I, v, 45), and Malvolio calls him "a barren rascal" (I, v, 90) whom an ordinary fool has put down in a battle of wits. Yet Olivia obviously regards Feste as sane when she insists that he read Malvolio's letter "i' thy right wits" (V, i, 305). We must forgive the lady's petulance and allow for the steward's spleen. Even without Viola's discerning comments, we may recognize the wise fool in Feste from some of his earliest lines: "Wit, an't be thy will, put me into good fooling! Those wits that think they have thee do very oft prove fools; and I that am sure I lack thee may pass for a wise man. For what says Quinapalus? 'Better a witty fool than a foolish wit' " (I, v, 35). This modest statement is but a change rung upon that old proverb which Touchstone quotes directly: "The fool doth think he is wise, but the wise man knows himself to be a fool" (*A.Y.L.* V, i, 34).

And yet Feste, unlike Touchstone, is not altogether pleased to be taken for a fool. It is one thing to feed the thin-faced knight's voracious appetite for nonsense; it is quite another to be misprized by the judicious. We have already noted his reply to the Lady Olivia that it is not the cowl that makes the monk (I, v, 62) or the suit of motley that makes the fool. In answer to Viola-Cesario's query, "Art not thou the Lady Olivia's fool?" Feste protests, "No, indeed, sir. The Lady Olivia has no folly. . . . I am indeed not her fool, but her corrupter of words" (III, i, 36). Nor will he let Sebastian have the last word in the misunderstanding over the youth's identity:

SEB. Go to, go to, thou art a foolish fellow. Let me be clear of thee.
CLOWN. Well held out, i' faith! No, I do not know you; nor I am not sent to you by my lady, to bid you come speak with her; nor your name is not Master Cesario; nor this is not my nose neither. Nothing that is so is so.
SEB. I prithee vent thy folly somewhere else. Thou know'st not me.

CLOWN. Vent my folly! He has heard that word of some great man, and now applies it to a fool. Vent my folly! (IV, i, 3)

His annoyance is assuaged only when Sebastian gives him money to be rid of him.

Gervinus is a bit too severe with Feste when he comments that "No other of Shakespeare's fools is so conscious of his superiority as this one."[12] A proper estimate would equate Feste with Aristotle's *eutrapelos*—the ready-witted man who knows his own worth but does not exaggerate it.[13] At times a tone of self-mockery rings through Feste's fooling. The fool strikes this note when, in making excuses to his mistress for his late truancy, he argues: "Bid the dishonest man mend himself: if he mend, he is no longer dishonest; if he cannot, let the botcher mend him. Anything that's mended is but patch'd; virtue that transgresses is but patch'd with sin, and sin that amends is but patch'd with virtue" (I, v, 49). In propounding a paradox to Duke Orsino, Feste reveals the self-knowledge of a Socrates:

DUKE. I know thee well. How dost thou, my good fellow?
CLOWN. Truly, sir, the better for my foes, and the worse for my friends.
DUKE. Just the contrary: the better for thy friends.
CLOWN. No, sir, the worse.
DUKE. How can that be?
CLOWN. Marry, sir, they praise me and make an ass of me. Now my foes tell me plainly I am an ass; so that by my foes, sir, I profit in the knowledge of myself, and by my friends I am abused; so that, conclusions to be as kisses, if your four negatives make your two affirmatives, why then, the worse for my friends and the better for my foes. (V, i, 11)

We may detect the fine Italian hand of *Dottore Graziano* in this logic-chopping and syllogism-mongering, but the effect of the argument goes beyond mere buffoonery.

Feste utters few of the wise saws which are the stock-in-trade of most professional fools. What wisdom he brings from Solomon's treasury he mints over into new coin. He even transmutes Cicero's *Stultorum plena sunt omnia*,[14] the staple of so many fool plays, into fresh currency when he observes, "Foolery, sir, does walk about the orb like the sun; it shines everywhere" (III, i, 43). Another aphorism which the fool twists to his own uses comes originally from The Sermon on the Mount: "And if the blind lead the blind, both shall fall into the ditch" (Matt. xv, 14). When Olivia asks Feste to take care of her drunken kinsman, the fool replies, "He is but mad yet, madonna, and the fool shall look to the madman"

(I, v, 145). On presenting Malvolio's letter to Olivia near the end of the play, Feste again puns on the old proverb:

OLI. Open't and read it.
CLOWN. Look then to be well edified, when the fool delivers the madman. (V, i, 297)[15]

But Feste's wit, we must allow, goes deeper than mere verbal felicity. Viola, who alone shares his awareness of life's contradictions, pays him the highest tribute ever bestowed upon a household jester:

> This fellow is wise enough to play the fool,
> And to do that well craves a kind of wit.
> He must observe their mood on whom he jests,
> The quality of persons, and the time;
> Not, like the haggard, check at every feather
> That comes before his eye. This is a practice
> As full of labour as a wise man's art;
> For folly that he wisely shows, is fit;
> But wise men, folly-fall'n, quite taint their wit.
> (III, i, 66)

This familiar passage has frequently been quoted as a comment on the fool's tact and complaisance. That he puts his art and fooling to shrewd uses cannot be denied. Feste is an inveterate beggar. He fools more money out of Duke Orsino than he earns by his singing. Even Sir Andrew parts with sixpence to put him in good fooling. And most of the other characters contribute toward the fool's maintenance. Like Shakespeare himself, Feste must live by his art.

But this fool puts his wise reflections on the frailty of his fellows to other uses. Although he makes his pleasantries pay him in cash, his motives are not wholly mercenary.[16] He practices his art for the pleasure it affords him. Feste thoroughly enjoys playing up to the Duke's romantic melancholy with a doleful song, as he proves by his farewell speech to Orsino. He too is "dog at a catch" and amuses himself with the foolish knight:

CLOWN. By'r lady, sir, and some dogs will catch well.
AND. Most certain. Let our catch be 'Thou knave.'
CLOWN. 'Hold thy peace, thou knave,' knight? I shall be constrained in't to call thee knave, knight.
AND. 'Tis not the first time I have constrained on to call me knave. Begin, fool. It begins, 'Hold thy peace.'
CLOWN. I shall never begin if I hold my peace. (II, iii, 64)

In ridiculing the simple gull Sir Andrew, the fool is far more artful than are Maria and the buffoonish Sir Toby. With a wry wink at his audience, he lets the thin-faced knight exhibit his own foolishness without comment.

Modern prejudices notwithstanding, Feste gives us some of his most delicious fooling in the gulling of the pharisaical Malvolio. One who reads the play soberly in the study may easily miss some of the fine absurdity in the scene wherein Feste slips in and out of the role of Sir Topas, the lenten preacher.

CLOWN. Alas, sir, how fell you besides your five wits?
MAL. Fool, there was never man so notoriously abus'd. I am as well in my wits, fool, as thou art.
CLOWN. But as well? Then you are mad indeed, if you be no better in your wits than a fool.
MAL. They have here propertied me; keep me in darkness, send ministers to me, asses, and do all they can to face me out of my wits.
CLOWN. Advise you what you say. The minister is here. –Malvolio, Malvolio, thy wits the heavens restore! Endeavour thyself to sleep and leave thy vain bibble babble.
MAL. Sir Topas!
CLOWN. Maintain no words with him, good fellow. –Who, I, sir? Not I, sir. God b' wi' you, good Sir Topas! –Marry, amen. –I will, sir, I will.
MAL. Fool, fool, fool, I say!
CLOWN. Alas, sir, be patient. What say you, sir? I am shent for speaking to you. (IV, ii, 90)

All that we can say to this *tour de force* of Feste's is "Amen. God rest your merry soul, fool."

Feste easily puts down Malvolio when the steward attempts some stiff-necked humor at the fool's expense:

OLI. What think you of this fool, Malvolio? Doth he not mend?
MAL. Yes, and shall do till the pangs of death shake him. Infirmity, that decays the wise, doth ever make the better fool.
CLOWN. God send you, sir, a speedy infirmity, for the better increasing your folly! (I, v, 79)

Mistress Mary is more evenly matched in her wits to the wise fool, but she also comes off second best in some of her encounters with him. The crafty minx is reduced to a surly "Peace, you rogue; no more o' that" (I, v, 32) when Feste uncovers her neat little scheme to ensnare Sir Toby. Besides, she is witty only on one level; whereas Feste moves easily and gracefully through all levels of the comedy. Maria, for instance, gives no indication that she is aware of the fatuity and comic absurdity of her mistress or the Duke Orsino.

At this point, the fool's wit, in the modern sense of the word, merges with wisdom. The clever jester passes into the wise fool as Feste comes to embody the comic spirit of the play. If *As You Like It* portrays and parodies the affectations of love in a forest, *Twelfth Night* contrasts simple and sentimental love in more urban surroundings. Shakespeare presents love in varying degrees and on several planes in *Twelfth Night*—ranging from the sentimental affectation of Orsino and the self-love of Malvolio to the genuine and enduring love of Viola. Feste, who moves upstairs and belowstairs and back and forth among the groups of assorted lovers, is our guide through the mazes of emotion. That Orsino and even Olivia are slightly ridiculous figures has not always been recognized. The Duke, whose "Love-thoughts lie canopied with bow'rs" (I, i, 41), is a sentimental sybarite. He is not in love with Olivia but with the sensations of love in himself. Olivia must suspect something of the sort when she rejects his suit, but Feste accurately anatomizes the Duke's absurdity: "Now, the melancholy god protect thee, and the tailor make thy doublet of changeable taffeta, for thy mind is a very opal! I would have men of such constancy put to sea, that their business might be everything, and their intent everywhere . . ." (II, iv, 75).

Olivia too is a sentimentalist, whose love is self-indulgence. She clings to an imagined grief for a brother dead seven years. Feste impudently twits her upon her immoderate sorrow:

CLOWN. Good madonna, why mourn'st thou?
OLI. Good fool, for my brother's death.
CLOWN. I think his soul is in hell, madonna.
OLI. I know his soul is in heaven, fool.
CLOWN. The more fool, madonna, to mourn for your brother's soul, being in heaven. Take away the fool, gentlemen. (I, v, 72)

Although Olivia and Orsino are alike in that their loves are grounded in vanity, they differ widely in the force of their feelings. The Duke deliberately cultivates his melancholy and his love languor; whereas the Countess allows her feelings to grow rank and unrestrained. We are not at all surprised to see her rush impulsively from inordinate grief for her brother to a no less exaggerated passion for Cesario. Feste suggests that whoever marries Olivia will not have an easy time of it after the wedding: "The Lady Olivia has no folly. She will keep no fool, sir, till she be married; and fools are as like husbands as pilchers are to herrings—the husband's the bigger" (III, i, 37).

Ironically it is Olivia and not the fool who comments upon Malvolio's self-love, although she is not wholly free of the disease herself. And Maria, arch-intriguer of the plot against Malvolio, observing "that it is his grounds of faith that all that look on him love him" (II, iii, 164), uses his vanity to contrive his fall. Malvolio unaided reveals the depths of his folly in love before he nibbles at Maria's bait. Finally, as a droll footnote to the whole affair, Feste comes in to plague Malvolio in his darkened cell, singing an old song:

CLOWN. 'Hey, Robin, jolly Robin
Tell me how thy lady does.'
MAL. Fool!
CLOWN. 'My lady is unkind, perdie!'
MAL. Fool!
CLOWN. 'Alas, why is she so?'
MAL. Fool, I say!
CLOWN. 'She loves another' —Who calls, ha? (IV, ii, 79)

And thus by his characteristic indirection, the wise fool merrily mocks the self-important steward.

Twelfth Night, the comedy saturated with some of Shakespeare's richest poetry, closes charmingly with Feste's song, "When that I was and a little tiny boy." Critics respond variously to this and the other incidental songs of the play. Sir Edmund Chambers presumably speaks for the majority opinion when he says that "the charming songs assigned to Feste the jester have no particular relation to the principal theme."[17] Most of us are content to leave the theatre humming over to ourselves the last lines which serve as an epilogue: "But that's all one, our play is done, / And we'll strive to please you every day" (V, i, 416). But one need not be too curious to believe that in the words of the final song Feste may be touching lightly but gracefully on one of the central ideas of the play. Surely the third stanza, with the lines: "But when I came, alas! to wive, / With hey, ho, the wind and the rain, / By swaggering could I never thrive, / For the rain it raineth every day" (V, i, 406), can be understood as Feste's wise reflection on the foolish lovers of the play. What could be more fitting than for the artful Feste to make his comment by way of a song?

Lavache, the Ribald Jester

Eric Partridge, who has a nose for such things, has detected less bawdiness in *Twelfth Night* than in any comparable play of Shakespeare's.[18] He might have added that Feste is freer than any other stage fool from wanton or indecent speech. No such claim, however, can be made for Lavache, the witty jester of *All's Well that Ends Well.* The face under the cap and bells is familiar, but the expression is somehow different. Feste's wry smile has turned to a leer in Lavache. More frequently than Shakespeare's other fools, he jokes about sex and chastity through sly innuendo. Touchstone, of course, makes the usual quips about cuckoldry, but his bawdiness is of an open, animal sort. In Lavache's defense of the wittol, there is something equivocal which seems to anticipate Middleton: "He that ears my land spares my team and gives me leave to inn the crop. If I be his cuckold, he's my drudge. He that comforts my wife is the cherisher of my flesh and blood; he that cherishes my flesh and blood loves my flesh and blood; he that loves my flesh and blood is my friend: ergo, he that kisses my wife is my friend" (I, iii, 47).[19] The least characteristic of Shakespeare's fools, Lavache most nearly resembles his non-Shakespearean contemporaries, Passarello, Dondolo, and Pickadill. He is closer to the sardonic Gelasimus and the railing Marcolf than is Touchstone or Feste.

Admittedly Lavache is less amiable and amusing than either of the two earlier fools. But is he merely the voice of vulgar cynicism in the play?[20] Is the Countess, his mistress, right when she calls him "a foul-mouth'd and calumnious knave" (I, iii, 60)? Several scenes later on, she exults, "I play the noble housewife with the time. / To entertain it so merrily with a fool" (II, ii, 62). No, the fool has become the innocent victim of guilt by association. He has been smirched by the same stroke that has tarnished the reputations of Parolles and Bertram. When he comments on the lack of chastity in women, Lavache is only assuming the traditional attitude of the satirical jester toward women: "And we might have a good woman born but for every blazing star, or at an earthquake, 'twould mend the lottery well. A man may draw his heart out ere 'a pluck one" (I, iii, 90). But even here the fool excepts Helena as the one good woman in ten. And elsewhere he expresses his admiration and affection for the young lady:

LAF. 'Twas a good lady, 'twas a good lady. We may pick a thousand sallets ere we light on such another herb.

CLOWN. Indeed, sir, she was the sweet marjoram of the sallet, or rather, the herb of grace. (IV, v, 14)

This speech does not sound like foul-mouthed calumny.

Lavache, like Touchstone, is a realist when it comes to love. His reason for marrying Isbel sounds suspiciously like Touchstone's excuse for marrying Audrey: "My poor body, madam, requires it. I am driven on by the flesh; and he must needs go that the devil drives" (I, iii, 30). Jaques predicts that Touchstone's "loving voyage" (*A.Y.L.* V, iv, 197) with Audrey will be but of two months' duration; Lavache himself confesses to a cooling ardor for Isbel: "I have no mind to Isbel since I was at court. Our old ling and our Isbels o' th' country are nothing like your old ling and your Isbels o' th' court. The brains of my Cupid's knock'd out, and I begin to love, as an old man loves money, with no stomach" (*All's W.* III, ii, 13). Read out of the context, this confession seems to brand the fool as a knave. But in the proper place, these lines would be absurdly irrelevant if they meant that and nothing more. We must remember that, while Lavache is confessing his waning love for Isbel, the Countess is reading a letter—a letter wherein Bertram flouts his marriage to Helena and proposes to forsake her. In this setting, the fool's confession becomes a sharp parody on Bertram's rejection of Helena. Lavache is a parodist, too. Like Touchstone, he uses himself and his mock love affair as the means of commenting ironically on the behavior of his betters. If his humor tastes a little sour now and then, the explanation may be that it is nourished on the unpleasant follies of Bertram and Parolles.

One may cavil at calling Lavache a wise fool, but one must agree that he is a conscious humorist. Even Parolles, the object of much of his scorn, admits that he is a witty fool (II, iv, 32). The Countess of Rossillion looks for entertainment and edification from her old jester, and he strives to give her a little of both. In addition to a penchant for parody, Lavache exhibits something of Feste's verbal virtuosity. And like Passarello, this fashionable fool delights in grotesque similes:

COUNT. Will your answer serve fit to all questions?
CLOWN. As fit as ten groats is for the hand of an attorney, as your French crown for your taffety punk, as Tib's rush for Tom's forefinger, as a pancake for Shrove Tuesday, a morris for May Day, as a nail to his hole, the cuckold to his horn, as a scolding quean to a wrangling knave, as a nun's lip to the friar's mouth, nay, as the pudding to his skin. (II, ii, 20)[21]

This kind of wit is likely to grow stale with time and changing manners. Lavache's wit is modish, and to the very degree that it was stylish and smart in his day it has become flat and somewhat tedious to us today.

"A shrewd knave and an unhappy" (IV, v, 66), comments Lafeu, and the description of Lavache is apt. Touchstone is a more thoughtful and Feste a gayer fool, but Lavache is a clever, urbane jester. He has his share of that human warmth and dignity which seems to be the birthright of so many of Shakespeare's characters. Even the discredited Parolles draws from him a mixture of pity and contempt at the last: "Pray you, sir, use the carp as you may; for he looks like a poor decayed, ingenious, foolish, rascally knave. I do pity his distress in my similes of comfort, and leave him to your lordship" (V, ii, 23). But Lavache, like most stage fools, is incidental to the plot of the play. He does not even contribute to the overthrow of Parolles. And he is unlike Shakespeare's other fools in that his role bears no significant relationship to the theme of *All's Well*. He is in no way a measure of the play's meaning, as are Touchstone, Feste, and Lear's Fool for their plays. Despite the valiant efforts of W. W. Lawrence and others to explain the meaning of *All's Well*, the play and its fool alike remain distasteful to most modern readers and audiences.

Lear's Fool and His Five Wits

The Fool in *King Lear* has become so enmeshed in the play's meaning that it is difficult to disentangle him. Several recent critics have approached the play's theme through the character of the Fool and the concept of wise folly which he brings into the play. One of these new critics, William Empson, refers to Lear's Fool as a lunatic.[22] But is this fool mentally defective? If the Fool and his 'folly' are so important to our full understanding of *King Lear*, then the question is not academic. Except for the bizarre diagnoses of a few scattered writers, the consensus of the critics is that Touchstone, Feste, and Lavache are clever artificial fools, not naturals; that they are conscious humorists, not unwitting instruments. However, when they come to examine Lear's Fool, the critics are far from agreed on the state of his mind. The preponderant opinion since the beginning of the nineteenth century seems to have been that this fool is a naive natural or even a half-wit boy. Coleridge speaks of his "grotesque prattling" and inspired idiocy.[23] An earlier commentator, Francis Douce (II, 169) calls him "a mere *natural* with a considerable share of cunning." And Boas sees in the working of the Fool's mind "that strange mixture of simplicity and acuteness which is so often the birthright of 'a natural.' "[24]

There is some justification for this reading of the Fool's character in the light of a confused popular tradition. Triboulet was little more than a babbling idiot who belonged successively to two French kings, yet he was endowed by the folk imagination with wisdom and intelligence far beyond the reach of his reason. Popular fancy is constantly distorting and disregarding the facts of history when building its legends. Shakespeare went not to history but to the popular and literary tradition (or to Armin, which was the same thing) for the stuff of which he created Feste and Lear's Fool, but the poet refined upon the fool of tradition. Even in conceiving his most ambiguous characters, Shakespeare was ever firm and dramatically sure. Can we say then that in his conception of Lear's Fool the dramatist abandoned his usual methods, that his fool wavered between an unconscious simpleton and a penetrating, ironical commentator? Since the best and only reliable arbiter in all such matters of interpretation is the text itself, let us turn to it.

Midway through the play, the disguised Edgar addresses the Fool as "innocent" (III, vi, 8). There is little to be gleaned from the context in which the term appears. However, in a passage which closely follows, there are speeches which strikingly contrast the Fool, the crazed King, and the feigned madman:

FOOL. Prithee, nuncle, tell me whether a madman be a gentleman or a yeoman.
LEAR. A king, a king!
FOOL. No, he's a yeoman that has a gentleman to his son; for he's a mad yeoman that sees his son a gentleman before him.
LEAR. To have a thousand with red burning spits
Come hizzing in upon 'em—
EDGAR. The foul fiend bites my back.
FOOL. He's mad that trusts in the tameness of a wolf, a horse's health, a boy's love, or a whore's oath. (III, vi, 10)

Of the three, the Fool alone speaks to the point, and he speaks the language of proverbial wisdom, the language of Marcolf. Edgar has as much and no more reason for calling Lear's Fool an "innocent" as Rosalind has for terming Touchstone a "natural." Both gentlefolk accept the gold coin for a copper penny, for so it passes current. As with the ambiguous title "Fool," the names "Innocent" and "Natural" seem to have been titles of office as frequently as they were descriptive epithets.

To settle this vexing problem of the sanity of Lear's Fool, we have only to contrast him with characters clearly meant to portray natural fools. If we listen to the characteristic drivel of Fancy, Ignorance, Lomia, or even Patch and then listen to the pointed rhymes and metaphors of Lear's Fool, the difference becomes immediately apparent. Frantyke Fansy-Seruyce in Skelton's morality *Magnyfycence* describes himself as a ninny:

Somtyme I laughe ouer lowde;
Somtyme I wepe for a gew gaw;
Somtyme I laughe at waggynge of a straw.
With a pere my loue you may wynne,
And ye may lese it for a pynne. (1013–1017)

Ignorance, in Redford's *Wyt and Science,* displays his folly not only in what he says but in how he says it. He is such a noddy that he babbles on and on about "a new cote," but he cannot dress himself without the help of Idleness, the Vice in the play (ll. 550–559). The female fool Lomia in *Common Conditions* obviously lacks her full complement of wits. She is labelled "a naturall" in the stage directions announcing her entrance, and she immediately sets about to prove the charge in a brief soliloquy:

My lady sayes and I will learne well and take heede,
She will giue me a trim velvet cap with a fether,
To put on my head against colde weather.
And my lady will make me a trim longe cote downe to the ground.
And if any wil mary mee, she wil giue him twenty and a hundred pound
My lady can dance, so shee can and I must learne to,
Else I shall neuer get me a husband, for all that euer I can do. . . . (ll. 1382–1388)

And Patch, in Rowley's chronicle play, is a vain but simple creature who is so enamored of fancy clothing that he will risk a beating to get a fine silk point for his hose. In reply to Summers' shrewd offer, he chortles, "O brave, O brave, give me it, cousin, and I'll do whatsoever 'tis" (p. 21, ed. Elze.). We may sympathize with poor Patch when the King dandles him up and down like a football, but we must admit that he is a ninny and an easy butt for Will Summers' trickery.

Paradoxically, Lear's Fool is nobody's fool. He seldom lapses into nonsense or irrelevance; when he does, he does so to save himself from a beating. The Fool obliquely taunts Goneril: "The hedge-sparrow fed the cuckoo so long / That it had it head bit off by it young" and then skips off into quasi-nonsense: "So out went the candle, and we were left darkling" (*Lear* I, iv, 235). This seemingly irrelevant last line may echo several verses from Spenser's version of the tale of Lear: "But true it is that, when the oyle is spent, / The light goes out, and weeke is throwne away; / So when he had resigned his regiment, / His daughter gan despise his drouping day, / And wearie wax of his continuall stay" (*F.Q.* II, x, 30). The similarity can hardly be coincidental when both passages refer to Goneril's treatment of Lear. A little further on the Fool makes another sharp thrust at Goneril but immediately blunts its effect with what sounds like the refrain from an old song: "May not an ass know when the cart draws the horse? / Whoop, Jug, I love thee!" (I, iv, 244). If we remember that "Jug" was not only a diminutive variant for Joan or Jane but was also a cant term for a common trull,[25] we are not at all sure that the exclamation is really pointless. Can it not be that the Fool uses this mock declaration of love and loyalty to Goneril merely to deride those turncoats and time-pleasers who, like Oswald, shift and veer with every wind of favor? Such an interpretation would fit some later speeches of the Fool as well. Certainly he does not expect the loyal Kent to heed his cynical advice to "Let go thy hold when a great wheel runs down a hill, lest it break thy neck with following it" (II, iv, 72). The Fool habitually hides his meaning in metaphor.

Another passage which has troubled the explicators combines paradox, metaphor, and a bit of proverbial lore:

> The codpiece that will house
> Before the head has any,
> The head and he shall louse:
> So beggars marry many.
> The man that makes his toe
> What he his heart should make
> Shall of a corn cry woe,
> And turn his sleep to wake. (III, ii, 27)

Commentators have noted the obvious reference in the first stanza to the imprudent behavior of beggars and its logical consequences, but they have not always remarked on the relevance of the Fool's gibe to Lear's plight. Furness explains that Lear in preferring Regan and Goneril to Cordelia is like the man who covers the meaner members of his body and leaves his head and heart unprotected and as a result suffers pinching and pain in those very parts he sought to protect.[26] A careful reading of this verse is not only rewarding in itself but will help to throw light upon a sequent passage. As Kent enters, the Fool remarks, "Marry, here's grace and a codpiece; that's a wise man and a fool" (III, ii, 40).[27] Grace is, of course, a gentleman, the King in this instance. Or has he, the wise man, by his irrational behavior toward Cordelia changed places with the Fool? Has he not acted the part of a codpiece covering and protecting those baser parts—his lecherous and ungrateful daughters, Goneril and Regan? The Fool suggests that it may be the King who is the real fool.

So well does he disguise his thoughtful comments in the veiled language of imagery and old songs that he has misled some observers into actually taking him for a fool. Such a misunderstanding does not disturb him any more than it troubles Touchstone. To Kent's grudging admission that "This is not altogether fool, my lord," the Fool responds with characteristic insouciance: "No, faith; lords and great men will not let me. If I had a monopoly out, they would have part on't. And ladies too, they will not let me have all the fool to myself; they'll be snatching" (I, iv, 166).[28] Critics

*
uses song like Feste, -> to cover up!

have been led astray not always by an unperceptive literal-mindedness but sometimes by a desire to superimpose their own patterns on Shakespeare's design. Coleridge speaks of "the overflowings of the wild wit of the Fool" (Raysor, II, 266), and Bradley complains that regarding the Fool in *Lear* as wholly sane "destroys the poetry of the character."[29] But whose poetry are we here considering—Coleridge's, Bradley's, or Shakespeare's? Shakespeare's conception of the timid but faithful fool, torn from his natural element—the banquet hall—and thrust shivering upon the wild, stormy heath is poetic enough for our imagination, particularly when we remember that the Fool follows his King against the promptings of his own common sense. He gives shrewd advice to others but does not heed it himself.

What becomes then of the "inspired idiot" of Coleridge's dramatic tableau (Raysor, II, 63)? Does the Fool tread some middle ground "between instinct and consciousness," such as Gervinus assigns to Touchstone (p. 403)? Is he not a little "touched in the brain"; "a quick-witted though not whole-witted lad"?[30] The paradox has more of poetry than truth in it. Many of the Fool's comments betray a shrewd knowledge of the world, not what one would expect from a brilliant half-wit:

> FOOL. O nuncle, court holy water in a dry house is better than this rain water out o' door. Good nuncle, in, and ask thy daughters blessings! Here's a night pities neither wise men nor fools. (III, ii, 10)

The Fool has wit enough to come out of the rain but is restrained by a stronger power—loyalty to his sick King. Which of his five wits does the Fool lack? Certainly he has abundant store of fantasy and imagination—else he would not be constantly speaking in metaphor. His memory is long as we may see from his continual harping upon Lear's past and his injustice to Cordelia. The Fool does not lack common sense. His urging the King to come to terms with his daughters and the shrewd but cynical advice he gives Kent prove that he sees the world as it is. The only one of his faculties about which there may be any doubt is his judgment. We have already noted how his loyalty gets the better of his common sense. That lapse may be construed as a weakness in judgment—if we adopt the point of view of Goneril.

What about the Fool's heckling the King into madness? An anonymous Gentleman tells Kent and us that the Fool "labours to outjest his [Lear's] heart-struck injuries" (III, i, 16). But, these very jests are neither wise nor psychologically sound when applied as remedy for Lear's malady. Nay, even more; they are downright harmful. Professor Campbell observes that the Fool's "jests, far from mitigating his master's woes, intensify them by forcing the King to realize the depth of his folly."[31] The Fool then bears some of the responsibility for driving Lear mad. From this observation, one might argue that Lear's Fool is either malicious or stupidly naive. What then are we to say of the behavior of Kent? No one has seriously questioned his loyalty to his King or his sanity. And yet Kent's rash and headstrong righteousness is equally unwise and injudicious as a physic for Lear's choleric temper. Bradley notes that it is Kent who brings Lear's quarrel with Goneril to a head, and in falling upon the detestable Oswald and beating him, "he provides Regan and Cornwall with a pretext for their inhospitality."[32] Kent therefore must share with the Fool any responsibility for hurrying Lear out of his wits. If Kent demonstrates by his loyal-hearted blundering that he has "more man than wit" (II, iv, 42) about him, then the Fool shows by his probing metaphors that he has no less of either quality. Both the Fool and the loyal Kent are too emotionally attached to the King to be good physicians to his sick mind.

About the Fool's doglike fidelity to Lear, a few further words are needful. Much has been written in praise of his utter, blind devotion to his master. Perhaps, we ought to recall, parenthetically, that the Fool wavers in his loyalty for a long moment and only hurries after his King when commanded by Goneril: "You, sir, more knave than fool, after your master!" Immediately afterwards he throws off all prudence and sings:

> A fox, when one has caught her,
> And such a daughter,
> Should sure to the slaughter,
> If my cap would buy a halter.
> So the fool follows after. (I, iv, 337, 340)

The incident should temper but not destroy our belief in the Fool's loyalty. Whether he follows Lear, at first, out of faithfulness or merely from necessity matters little. He follows and stays with his master until forced to drop out of the play. And in remaining by Lear, the Fool violates his own sense of prudence. If this is not devotion, it is the next best thing. Walking clear-eyed into the stormy night and to his probable death on the heath, he comes as close as any fool ever does to the heroic.

With the prophetic sense so often attributed to fools and madmen, Lear's Fool sings a stave and makes a prediction:

> That sir which serves and seeks for gain,
> And follows but for form,
> Will pack when it begins to rain

And leave thee in the storm.
But I will tarry; the fool will stay,
And let the wise man fly.
The knave turns fool that runs away;
The fool no knave, perdy. (II, iv, 79)

The first part of this jingle is a clear forecast of the course of the play and of the Fool's relation to it. The last two lines, however, have caused some confusion. That eminent rationalist, Dr. Samuel Johnson, solved the problem by emending the text to read: "The fool turns knave, that runs away; / The knave no fool, ——."[33] But, although his revision makes easier reading, it is too pedestrian for the Fool's meaning. Johnson's changed reading not only alters the words but rudely violates the character and spirit of Shakespeare's wise fool. It is the sort of shrewdly cynical observation that a Will Summers or a Lavache might have made, not the Fool of Lear. The ironical fool is playing ambiguously with the term "fool." The knave who runs away from a friend in adversity is accounted prudent, even wise, in the eyes of the world and such worldlings as Goneril, Regan, and Edmund. But he is no more than a fool in the eyes of God, for, as Saint Paul says, "the wisdom of this world is foolishness with God" (I Cor. iii, 18). The Fool emphatically declares that he is no such knave, and we are left to infer that he may be truly wise in the sight of God.

This fool has come a long way from the railing Marcolf and the scheming Cacurgus. How far he has progressed beyond his shrewd ancestors and his cunning contemporaries may be seen in the almost contemptuous twist which he gives to the prudential wisdom of Solomon. When he cynically advises Kent: "We'll set thee to school to an ant, to teach thee there's no labouring i' th' winter" (II, iv, 68), he is echoing:

Go to the ant, thou sluggard;
Consider her ways, and be wise:
Which having no chief,
Overseer, or ruler,
Provideth her bread in the summer,
And gathereth her food in the harvest.
(Prov. vi, 6)

But he does not really wish Kent to follow his advice, for as he remarks a little later, "I would have none but knaves follow it, since a fool gives it" (II, iv, 77). He has become a wise fool in the Erasmian or Pauline sense.

The Fool has also become Lear's alter ego, his externalized conscience, or, as he puts it himself, "Lear's shadow" (I, iv, 251). In this role he chides the King:

FOOL. If thou wert my fool, nuncle, I'ld have thee beaten for being old before thy time.
LEAR. How's that?
FOOL. Thou shouldst not have been old till thou hadst been wise. (I, v, 44)

It is his task with his probing, sometimes caustic comments to cut away the cataracts of illusion which cloud Lear's eyes. What though the process be painful! What though the Fool, and later Edgar, must lead the old King through the darkness of unreason! The cure begun by the Fool is completed by Edgar and Cordelia, and Lear sees better through the eyes of a chastened spirit. The Fool's manner grows gentler as the King's madness increases. But it is not his business, nor has he the skill, to nurse the old man back to mental health. And so he goes to bed at noon in the play.

Granville-Barker justly warns that the Fool ought not to be "all etherealized by the higher criticism." The actor who plays the role must still "sing like a lark, juggle his words so that the mere skill delights us, and tumble around with all the grace in the world."[34] Such is the professional duty of the court and stage fool. But he must be so portrayed that we may perceive the Fool's real wisdom and the central position he takes in the meaning of the play. Shakespeare, by giving him another stanza to sing from Feste's old song, links this fool with the wise fool of comedy but at the same time points up the difference between the two. Lear's Fool has had to learn patience in adversity.

He that has and a little tiny wit—
With hey, ho, the wind and the rain—
Must make content with his fortunes fit,
For the rain it raineth every day. (III, ii, 74)

Although it would be a mistake to regard Shakespeare's fools as mere personifications of wisdom, it is nevertheless true that each possesses his special virtue. Touchstone, by the air of realism which he breathes into the antique forest of romance, may be said to embody the Aristotelian virtue of truthfulness. Feste, by his advocacy of moderation in loving and laughing, adds to truthfulness the virtue of temperance. He lives in and expresses the golden mean. Lear's Fool, however, transcends his fellows in the quality of his wisdom. He is the supremely wise fool who expresses in his heartfelt devotion to Cordelia and to his king the Christian virtues of patience, humility, and love.

Chapter V. CRITIC IN MOTLEY

"THERE IS NO SLANDER in an allow'd fool, though he do nothing but rail" (*Twel.* I, v, 101), observes Olivia; but the Malvolios who have smarted under the trenchant satire of professional fools are not so sure. Princes of the church and state must have winced more than once at the *sotties* and farces of the *Sociétés Joyeuses.* Pope Julius II was the target of several pointed burlesques of Pierre Gringoire. And performances of the *Enfants de Bon-Temps* were proscribed for a time after members of this Genevan fool society overstepped the bounds of political propriety and staged a lampoon on the ruling House of Savoy.[1] The next *sotties* that this group produced were in a subdued key. From the beginning of his career on the stage, the man in motley has been admirably suited to the role of satirical commentator. His traditional license to speak unwelcome truths and to comment freely upon the other characters and the action of the play makes the artificial fool a natural mouthpiece for satire. The melancholy hero of *Antonios Revenge* (c. 1599) knows exactly what he is doing when he disguises himself "in a fooles habit, with a little toy of a walnut shell, and sope, to make bubbles," for says he of the fool: "O, he hath a patent of immunities / Confirm'd by custome, seald by pollicie, / As large as spatious thought" (IV, i, 13, and stage direction). It is the fool's liberty, "as large a charter as the wind, to blow on whom I please" (*A.Y.L.* II, vii, 47), that makes Shakespeare's Jaques hanker after a coat of motley.

Malcontent and Buffoonish Satirists

Of course, Jaques and Antonio are not satirical fools but malcontent satirists, fellows of a very different stripe. Their urge to speak invective springs from a far different spirit from the humorous objectivity that animates the witty fool. Before returning to our discussion of the wise fool as a satirical commentator, we might do well to examine more fully those other commentators, the malcontent satirist and the railing buffoon, to see wherein they differ from our critic in motley.

Here is the way in which Marston's Pietro characterizes the malcontent Malevole:

This *Malevole* is one of the most prodigious affections that ever converst with nature; a man or rather a monster; more discontent then Lucifer when he was thrust out of the presence, his appetite is unsatiable as the Grave; as farre from any content as from heaven, his highest delight is to procure others vexation, and therein hee thinkes he truly serves heaven; for tis his position, whosoever in this earth can be contented is a slave and dam'd; therefore do's he afflict al in that to which they are most affected; the Elements struggle within him; his own soule is at variance: (within her selfe), his speach is halter-worthy at all howers. (*Malc.* I, ii, 17)

A gentleman of such kidney (or should we say spleen?) becomes a bitter satirist out of a genuine or an affected melancholy humor or from mere envy at the good fortune of others. Jonson's Carlo Buffone presents Macilente as an envious satirist in a sharp profile:

. . . a leane mungrell, he lookes as if he were chap-falne, with barking at other mens good fortunes: 'ware how you offend him, he carries oile and fire in his pen, will scald where it drops: his spirit's like powder, quick, violent: hee'le blow a man vp with a jest. . . . (I, ii, 212)[2]

Macilente does his best to live up to this bad opinion of his character. He is a railing satirist and a malicious wit-intriguer throughout the play.

Though he may have been modeled in part upon Macilente, Jaques is a much less caustic critic of his fellows. Much ink has been spilt and much nonsense uttered in the attempt to prove him a profound or sardonic philosopher. One editor of the play discovers in him the reflection of a disillusioned Shakespeare.[3] Professor Stoll has attempted to prove Jaques' kinship with Marston's Feliche and Malevole.[4] But it has remained for Dr. Z. S. Fink to reduce him to a type of ridiculous impostor then current in England—the malcontent traveler or Italianate Englishman.[5] Of course, Shakespeare gives us much more than a mere caricature in Jaques, else he would have amused but not have charmed us so. Like Orsino, he is a figure of high, not vulgar, comedy, but at bottom he is ridiculous. Rosalind sketches his type in all its fantasticality:

Farewell, Monsieur Traveller. Look you lisp and wear strange suits, disable all the benefits of your own country, be out of love with your nativity and almost chide God for making you that countenance you are; or I will scarce think you have swam in a gundello. (*A.Y.L.* IV, i, 33)

Shakespeare had already given his playgoers a voluble traveler in Don Armado, who affects to be "besieged with sable-coloured melancholy" (*L.L.L.* I, i, 233). And his young Prince Arthur, while ruminating on his own misfortunes, recalls those other young gentlemen who "would be as sad as night / Only for wantonness" (*John* IV, i, 15).

Jaques' "most humorous sadness" (*A.Y.L.* IV, i, 20) is partly a pose and partly a psychological reality. His humour, as Professor Campbell points out, corresponds to the symptoms ascribed by Elizabethan psychologists to the phlegmatic person turned unnaturally melancholic.[6] If, as the Duke asserts, Jaques has been a libertine, that circumstance could explain the adustion of his humor and his sour attitude toward the lovers in the play. It would also justify the severity of the Duke's rebuke:

> Most mischievous foul sin, in chiding sin.
> For thou thyself hast been a libertine,
> As sensual as the brutish sting itself;
> And all th' embossed sores and headed evils
> That thou with license of free foot has caught,
> Wouldst thou disgorge into the general world.
> (*A.Y.L.* II, vii, 64)

The spectacle of a reformed rake offering to "Cleanse the foul body of th' infected world" (II, vii, 60) is more than merely ludicrous. To the Duke, Jaques' satirical motives are impure, and his sincerity is, therefore, suspect. The thoroughgoing cynicism with which Jaques indicts the seven ages of man spoils the effectiveness of the piece as satire.[7] Such misanthropy mingled with scorn as Jaques flaunts in the face of the world is exactly what we should expect from the malcontent satirist.

The intemperate and scornful language that these satirists use reminds us of yet another kind of commentator–the railing buffoon or scurrilous tavern-jester. This type may best be seen in Jonson's Carlo Buffone or in Shakespeare's Thersites. Carlo is depicted by Macilente as:

> . . . an open-throated, black-mouth'd curre,
> That bites at all, but eates on those that feed him.
> A slaue, that to your face will (serpent-like)
> Creepe on the ground, as he would eate the dust;
> And to your backe will turne the taile, and sting
> More deadly then a scorpion. . . . (*E.M.O.* I, ii, 231)[8]

In Carlo, Jonson combines the alehouse jester, who knows no decorum of time or place or person and will "spare no sulphurous iest" (V, v, 28), with the malicious detractor, who delights in wounding others with his tongue. Quite appropriately, the old knight Puntarvolo seals up his venomous mouth with wax.

Thersites, too, according to the aged Nestor, is a scurrilous knave and backbiter: "A slave whose gall coins slanders like a mint, / To match us in comparisons with dirt" (*Troi.* I, iii, 193). It is hard to see how Professor Drayton Henderson could so far misunderstand Erasmus and Shakespeare as to describe the coarse jester of *Troilus and Cressida* as an Erasmian wise fool.[9] He is not to be confused with the witty professional fool. Although Achilles does speak of Thersites as "a privileg'd man" (II, iii, 61) and Ulysses states that "Achilles hath inveigled his (Ajax's) fool from him" (II, iii, 100), such remarks may be applied with equal justice to the clever servus or the cowardly buffoon of Greek and Roman drama. If he is sometimes called "fool" by the other characters in the play, that fact may be explained by the circumstance that Shakespeare must translate an earlier, traditional role into terms familiar to his Elizabethan audiences. Thersites wears no bells or bauble, nor does he sprinkle his wit with nonsense in the customary manner of the court or stage fool. Shakespeare, in his conception of the scurrilous Greek, may have been influenced, as Professor Campbell suggests, by Jonson's Carlo Buffone.[10] Certainly Thersites' mordant metaphors are reminiscent of Carlo's "stabbing *simile's*" (*E.M.O.* IV, iv, 114).

Thersites' favorite target for ridicule, after Ajax, seems to have been Patroclus. In a torrent of invective, he reviles Achilles' " male varlet": "thou idle immaterial skein of sleave silk, thou green sarcenet flap for a sore eye, thou tassel of a prodigal's purse, . . . Ah, how the poor world is pest'red with such waterflies–diminutives of nature!" (*Troi.* V, i, 35) And in the curses he heaps upon Patroclus, Thersites reminds us of Macilente.

> Now the rotten diseases of the South, the guts-griping, ruptures, catarrhs, loads o' gravel i' th' back, lethargies, cold palsies, raw eyes, dirt-rotten livers, whissing lungs, bladders full of imposthume, sciaticas, limekilns i' th' palm, incurable boneache, and the rivelled fee simple of the tetter, take and take again such preposterous discoveries! (*Troi.* V, i, 20)

Few characters can match Thersites in the muddy but turbulent stream of billingsgate that pours forth through the loose spigot of his mouth. Such abusive language, especially when unprovoked, is characteristic of the railing buffoon.

Shakespeare's Thersites differs in no essential way from Homer's; he is merely brought on the stage and rendered dramatically credible. Homer, with the help of Chapman, describes him in a passage from the *Iliad:*

> Thersites only would speak all. A most disorder'd store
> Of words he foolishly pour'd out, of which his mind held more

Than it could manage; anything, with which he could procure
Laughter, he never could contain. He should have yet been sure
To touch no kings; t'oppose their states becomes not jesters parts.[11]

Homer's ugly, malformed Thersites, like Shakespeare's, has a bitter, sarcastic tongue that knows no measure and is careless of the person on whom it jests. Both creatures fit Aristotle's definition of the buffoon: "the slave of his own sense of humour; he will spare neither himself nor anybody else, if he can raise a laugh, and he will use such language as no person of refinement would use or sometimes even listen to."[12] Theophrastus, as might be expected, follows Aristotle in condemning the buffoon for his excessive and unseemly jesting: "the Buffoon is one that will lift his shirt in the presence of free-born women; and at the theatre will applaud when others cease, hiss actors whom the rest of the audience approves, and raise his head and hiccup when the house is silent, so that he may make the spectators look round."[13]

Latin authors are no less severe in rejecting the buffoon and his coarse jesting. Cicero, however, is perfectly ready to laugh at the buffoon (*sannio*) in the proper place—at the theatre: "can there be anything so droll as a pantaloon [buffoon]? Yet it is for his face, his grimaces, his mimicry of mannerisms, his intonation, and in fact his general bearing, that he is laughed at. Humorous I am able to call him, but humorous for a low comedian, and not in the sense in which I would have an orator humorous."[14] Horace, as we have already noted, takes some pleasure in professional buffoons (*scurrae*). Apparently, a class of professional jesters flourished in Athens and Rome who enjoyed a license similar to that later accorded the medieval fool. The comedies of Plautus and Terence abound with such privileged creatures. Whatever distaste classical writers feel for the unsavory parasite stems from his unmannerliness rather than from his immorality.

When the Elizabethan Thomas Wilson discusses jesting and jesters in his *The Arte of Rhetorique* (1560), he adopts the Aristotelian attitude toward buffoonery. Wilson would have his readers "auoyd all grosse bourding, and alehouse iesting, but also to eschue all foolish talke, and Ruffine maners, such as no honest eares can once abide, nor yet any wittie man can like well or allowe" (p. 138).[15] And Thomas Lodge, although he gives a severely moral cast to his characters by labelling them fiends and "Devils Incarnat," embodies only the Aristotelian vice of excessive jesting in his character of "Immoderate and Disordinate Ioy." Lodge's jester is also akin to Theophrastus' character of the buffoon, only more particularized and set capering in the late sixteenth century.

. . . this fellow in person is comely, in apparell courtly, but in behauiour a very ape, and no man: his studie is to coine bitter ieasts, or to show antique motions, or to sing baudie sonnets and ballads: giue him a little wine in his head, he is Cōtinually flearing and making mouthes: he laughes intemperately at euery litle occasion, and dances about the house, leaps ouer tables, outskips mens heads, trips vp his companions héeles, burns Sacke with a candle, and hath all the feats of a Lord of misrule in the countrie: féed him in his humor, you shall haue his heart.[16]

Of course, Elizabethan dramatists need not have gone to nondramatic sources at all, as the stage buffoon was currently popular in Italy. His type has been fleering and flouting on the stages of the world from the time of Aristophanes.

Though Carlo Buffone and Thersites may be traced ultimately to the parasitical buffoon of classical inspiration, they have at least one trait which links them with medieval English tradition. In Macilente's description of Carlo and in Shakespeare's characterization of Thersites, chief stress seems to be placed upon the buffoon as a backbiter or maliciously witty detractor. There is a trace of this trait in Aristotle's definition: "he will spare neither himself *nor anybody else* [ed. ital.]." And Homer goes on to say of Thersites: "He most of all envied / Ulysses and Aecides, whom still his spleen would chide" (*Iliad* Bk. II, ll. 189 f., tr. Chapman). But there is not much asperity or moral opprobrium attached to the vice of envy in the writings of the ancients. Plato even regards envy and the painful feeling it engenders as necessary parts to a sense of the ridiculous.[17]

To the medieval Christian apologists, however, Envy is second only to Pride in the catalogue of the Seven Deadly Sins. A sin which can bring a human soul to perdition is far from being funny. Therefore a profane jester who personifies the spirit of envy is properly treated with loathing, not with laughter, in the writings of medieval Englishmen. That gentle-spirited cleric who addressed himself to a small group of anchoresses at the beginning of the thirteenth century gives us an effective portrait of the envious man or backbiter:

There are some Jesters who know of no other means of exciting mirth but to make wry faces, and distort their mouth, and scowl with their eyes. This art the unhappy, envious man practiseth in the devil's court, to excite to laughter their envious Lord. For, if any one saith or doeth well, they cannot, by any means, look that way with the direct eye of a good heart; but wink in another direction, and look on the left hand, and obliquely: and if there is anything to blame or dislike, there they scowl with both eyes; and when they hear of any good, they hang down both their ears, but their desire of evil is ever wide open. Then they distort their mouth, when they turn good to evil; and if there is somewhat of evil, they distort it, and make it worse by detraction.[18]

If Jonson and Shakespeare did not know the *Ancren Riwle*, they knew the sturdy English that runs through it and the later homilies and moralities.

The malcontent satirist and the bitter buffoon often adopt a tone that is too severe or too scurrilous for the targets of their ridicule, or else the types of folly they attack are too vicious for mere taunting. The disproportion between the matter and the manner of their comments is only too apparent. However justified Thersites may be in excoriating Patroclus or Ajax, he has no sufficient reason to turn loose his invective on Nestor, Ulysses, and Agamemnon. He uses too much acid in etching their portraits.

THER. . . . the policy of those crafty swearing rascals—that stale old mouse-eaten dry cheese, Nestor, and that same dog-fox, Ulysses—is not prov'd worth a blackberry. (*Troi.* V, iv, 10)

. . . .

Here's Agamemnon, an honest fellow enough and one that loves quails, but he has not so much brain as earwax . . . (V, i, 55)

On the other hand, the buffoon dismisses the nine years' siege of Troy a little too frivolously: "All the argument is a whore and a cuckold—a good quarrel to draw emulous factions and bleed to death upon" (II, iii, 77). Dramatists of Shakespeare's day were only too willing to commit their satirical comments to the tongues of buffoons and bitter malcontents.[19] Even the witty fools in several plays of the period speak with the insolence and ribaldry of tavern-jesters; but the best of them temper their impertinence with irony.

Satire on Morals

As we have noted earlier, the all-licensed fool frequently acts as a critic of contemporary life, courtly and ecclesiastical. Folie lets fly at the abuses of all three estates, as he presents fools' caps to the vicious representatives of each of the social classes. To the tyrannical prince he presents:

Ane nobill cap imperiell,
Quhilk is nocht ordanit bot for doings
Of Empreours, of Duiks and Kings,
For princelie and imperiall fuillis:
That sould haue luggis als lang as Muillis.

The pryde of Princes, withoutin faill,
Gars all the warld rin top ovir taill.
To win them warldlie gloir and gude,
Thay cure nocht schedding of saikles blude.
(*Ane Satyre*, ll. 4555–4563)

In reproving the arrogance of Emperor Charles V of Germany, Will Summers uses a gentler, more ironical tone, reminding him of the transiency of earthly glory and the democracy of the grave.

EMP. What say you to this, William?
An emperor is great
High is his seat,
Who is his foe?
WILL. The worms that shall eat
His carcass for meat,
Whether he will or no.[20]

Dondolo charges that the Duke of Urbino wishes to "play the foole himselfe alone without any rivall" (*Fawne* IV, i, 227), but he draws up no bill of particulars. Touchstone refers guardedly to the tyranny of the usurping Duke Frederick and is warned that he will "be whipp'd for taxation one of these days" (*A.Y.L.* I, ii, 91). But the witty fools that we are considering seldom tax the princes of the temporal state.[21]

However, these same court fools do not hesitate to criticize the lords spiritual for their hypocrisy and avarice. Folie reserves his sharpest barbs for those princes of the church who combine in themselves the follies and vices of the state and the clergy.

The Paip with bombard, speir, and scheild,
Hes send his armie to the feild.
Sanct Peter, Sanct Paull nor Sanct Androw,
Raisit never sic ane Oist I trow.
Is this fraternall charitie
Or furious folie, Quhat say ye?
Thay leird nocht this at Christis Scuillis:
Thairfoir I think them verie fuillis.
(*Ane Satyre*, ll. 4578–4585)

In a more subtle vein, Feste derides all clerical impostors.

MARIA. Nay, I prithee, put on this gown and this beard; make him [Malvolio] believe thou art Sir Topas the curate; do it quickly. I'll call Sir Toby the whilst.

CLOWN. Well, I'll put it on, and I will dissemble myself in't, and I would I were the first that ever dissembled in such a gown. (*Twel.* IV, ii, 1)

Lavache, on the other hand, singles out Puritan arrogance and hypocrisy as the targets for his satirical shafts.

CLOWN. Though honesty be no Puritan, yet it will do no hurt. It will wear the surplice of humility over the black gown of a big heart. (*All's W.* I, iii, 97)

Cardinal Wolsey, as the archetype of priestly avarice and chicanery, is the butt of more than one satirical fool. Folly in Skelton's *Magnyfycence* probably has the prelate in mind when he taunts "Such dawys, what soeuer they be, that be set in auctorite" (ll. 1243–1244). W. W. Greg, who believes that Skelton also wrote the interlude *Godly Quene Hester*, sees a lampoon on Wolsey in the person of the arrogant Aman.[22] But it is Will Summers of Samuel Rowley's play who most thoroughly exposes the Cardinal in all his duplicity. Rowley dramatizes a reported episode which reaches us from an independent source as well.[23] According to the old tale, Will visits the Cardinal's fool Patch and is entertained by him in Wolsey's wine cellar. When they attempt to tap a hogshead, they let loose a stream, not of wine but of gold coins. The two fools break open barrel after barrel only to find them all full of the hoarded wealth that the Cardinal has extorted from the people. In the presence of the King, Will shames Wolsey by his disclosures.

KING. Is his wine turned into gold, Will?
WOL. The fool mistakes, my gracious sovereign.
WILL. Ay, ay, my lord, ne'er set your wit to the fool's: Will Summers will be secret now and say nothing; if I would be a blab of my tongue, I could tell the king how many barrels full of gold and silver there was: six tuns filled with plate and jewels, twenty great trunks with crosses, crosiers, copes, mitres, maces, golden crucifixes, besides the four hundred and twelve thousand pound that the poor chimneys paid for Peter pence. But this is nothing, for when you are pope, you may pardon yourself for more knaveries than this comes to. (*When You See Me*, p. 72)

Using his license to the full, Will jeers at Henry's title of "Defender of the Faith." At this point, the witty fool becomes an instrument of the Protestant Rowley's hatred of popery.

WILL. I am sure the true faith is able to defend itself without thee, and as for the pope's faith—good faith! 'tis not worth a farthing, and therefore give him not a penny. (p. 25)

But this speech is not typical of the wise fool; it is not even characteristic of Rowley's fool. It is the presumption of the Cardinal, not his false doctrine, that Summers mocks at chiefly. In contest with the Cardinal, Will easily caps Wolsey's rhymes:

WOL. Well, Will, I'll try your rhyming wits once more: what say you to this:—

The bells hang high,
And loud they cry,
What do they speak?

WILL. If you should die,
There's none would cry,
Though your neck should break.

WOL. You are something bitter, William; but come on once more, I am for ye:—

A rod in school,
A whip for a fool,
Is always in season.

WILL. A halter and a rope
For him that would be pope
Against all right and reason. (p. 39)[24]

In addition to preying upon priestly hypocrisy and greed and princely arrogance, satirists have often grappled with wantonness, especially in women. The formal satirists, both in Rome and renaissance England, have frequently sunk their sharp fangs into the soft vice of lechery. The stage fool, too, as a part of his heritage from medieval satire and drama, takes a cynical view of women. The Marcolf of the German *Fastnachtspiel* and the later Latin *Sapientia Solomonis* apparently brings with him from the medieval *Collationes* a traditional cynicism toward women as lewd creatures. In the version of the play acted before Queen Elizabeth in 1565, a Marcolf in motley scurrilously rails on a strumpet, contrasting her viciousness with the innocence of a dead child.

MAR. I am a physiognomist. The child's eyes are now closed in sleep; you, wretch, are on the watch for young men. You open your door, strumpet, even before they knock; your door is closed to no one. If they do not come to you of their own accord, you attract them by coaxing and evil allure gleaming from your very eyes. Fie upon you, shameless wench! (*Sapientia Solomonis* III, iv, 29)

. . . .

> Yours is this dead baby here and you know my reasons for saying so. This baby has a head covered with flaxen hair; you conceal wrinkles under your paint. When you are old, withered, squalid, humped over, rough, with a foul weazel-colored skin, you will still wish to seem scarcely fifteen years old to your lovers. (III, iv, 55)

No other professional fool speaks so scornfully in reviling vicious men or women. Marcolf's withering tone is like that of Marston's early formal satires or the tirades of Malevole. The fool Gelasimus, in taunting Herodias, is more restrained and ironical in his language.

> HER. Do you not know me? Take that box on the ear.
> GEL. I know you better than I wish. You are Philip's wife.
> HER. Ha! Give me the other cheek. There, take that, and beware. Do not be mad enough to blab such things.
> GEL. Alas, truth ever begets hatred, and blows as well! As long as I live I will never again speak the truth.
> HER. Now tell whose I am.
> GEL. The wife of Herod.
> HER. But of which?
> GEL. Come hither. I will explain, and whisper it in your ear. You, who are the wife of Antipas, were formerly that of Philip. (*Archipropheta* IV, ii, 27)

Marston's Passarello carries on this traditional satire on women—but with a difference. There is always a suggestion that he is amused and a little attracted by the vice that he reprehends. We can excuse his impudently chiding the ladies of the court for their overuse of cosmetics.

> BILI. Didst thou see Madam *Floria* to-day?
> PAS. Yes, I found her repairing her face to-day, the red upon the white shewed as if her cheekes should have beene served in for two dishes of Barbaries in stewed broth, and the flesh to them a woodcocke. (*Malc.* III, i, 138)
>
> . . . .
>
> . . . she were an excellent Lady, but that hir face peeleth like Muscovie glasse. (I, vii, 130)

But there is something decidedly distasteful and equivocal about Passarello's mocking at courtly lasciviousness.

With the possible exception of Passarello and Dondolo, who seem to lie a little outside the tradition, the wise fool is easily distinguishable from the buffoonish railer or the malcontent satirist. Even when he speaks as a satirist, the fool prefers to make his comments by indirection. He voices his criticism by innuendo, parody, and the apposite recitation of old songs.

The wise fool is at once more particular and more penetrating in his criticism than is the formal satirist. Using the keener scalpel of comic irony, he dissects and anatomizes the permanent follies and affectations of his fellow man. He seldom concerns himself with those social or political abuses which arouse the spleen of most satirists. Instead he is constantly looking for the silly man behind the humorous or hurtful institution.

Satire on Social Affectation

By his very nature then, the wise or witty fool lends himself to the milder forms of social criticism—to the satire of humorous or affected types and to occasional lampoons on literature. The gallery of gulls and pretenders has grown in numbers and variety since Aristophanes' day. The architects of Cloudcuckootown are interrupted in their labors by several kinds of troublemakers: an oracle-monger, a geometrician, a political informer, and a dithyrambic poet, all in their separate ways trying to subvert the commonwealth.[25] Roman comedy thrived mostly on the follies of the braggart soldier and the hungry parasite and on the stock situations in which these stock characters found themselves. In renaissance Italy and England, comic dramatists altered and fused the old types and brought forth new forms of the preposterous pretender. The blustering and bumptious Thraso is supplanted by the elegant Spanish Captain.[26] And the alchemist emerges as a fresh variant on the quack-philosopher or learned charlatan.[27] But whatever their local habitation and names, these ludicrous figures have something in common—their absurd pretensions. Such men are ridiculous, as Plato observed long ago (*Philebus* 48–50), because of their vain conceits of beauty, wisdom, or virtue which they lack. Jonson's gulls stand forth in all their empty affectation when seen against the shadow of the renaissance gentleman whose manners they try to ape.[28]

Those who affect to be much wiser than they are have always appeared ridiculous. Sir John Davies, in his Second Epigram, has neatly pinned down these wriggling creatures for us: "But to define a Gull in termes precise, –/ A Gull is he which seemes, and is not wise."[29] The pedant or learned quack has waddled across the stage to the moderate amusement of spectators for the past twenty two hundred years. Solemn proud schoolmasters, from Lampriskos of Herodes' *Didaskalos* (Mime III, ll. 58–70) to Shakespeare's Holofernes and Sir Hugh Evans, have aroused scornful laughter at their vain mouthing of learned nonsense. Pseudo-philosophers, astrologers, and pretenders to occult knowledge have been fair game for comic playwrights from Epicharmus to Ben Jonson. The dolts Sordido, of *Every Man Out*, and Weatherwise, of Middleton's *No Wit, no Help*

Like a Woman's, who make love or harvest crops by the almanac, are almost lineal descendants of Aristophanes' Socrates. Sometimes these charlatans and bumptious fools have been allowed to reveal the depths of their own stupidity; at other times a clever slave or rustic has called attention to their inanities. In the plays we are considering, it is the wise fool who confounds the foolish wits of the gulls and impostors.

A type of presumptuous person who sometimes amused but more often annoyed Elizabethan playgoers was the social upstart. The pushing citizen and the parvenu courtier were persistent butts of dramatic and formal satire during the last decade of the sixteenth century. Conservative Englishmen laughed at them loud and scornfully, but perhaps a trifle nervously.[30] Try as he might to laugh or hoot him off the stage, Feste and his contemporaries must have heard Malvolio's parting shot uneasily: "I'll be reveng'd on the whole pack of you!" (*Twel.* V, i, 386)[31] Many of the playwrights of the day particularize their disapproval and depict the upstart as a Puritan, but Shakespeare prefers not to label his impostor too precisely. Instead, he makes his Malvolio into a universal type of arrogant presumption and time-pleasing hypocrisy.[32]

For his irreligion masking as sober piety, Feste, in the guise of Sir Topas, taunts Malvolio: "Fie, thou dishonest Satan! I call thee by the most modest terms; for I am one of those gentle ones that will use the devil himself with courtesy" (IV, ii, 35). Feste then intones a solemn little sermon: "Madman, thou errest. I say there is no darkness but ignorance, in which thou art more puzzled than the Egyptians in their fog" (IV, ii, 46). We may reasonably question whether the simile of "the Egyptians in their fog" in this particular context is pure, irrelevant nonsense. The allusion, of course, is to the plague which Moses calls down upon Pharaoh and the people of Egypt when they try to keep the Israelites as slaves and to hinder their setting forth to freedom in their own land (Ex. x, 21). Malvolio like Pharaoh temporarily humbles himself, but on being released from the dark house he too hardens his heart and becomes as unregenerate as ever. Set down in this literal fashion, such a reading of Feste's Biblical allusion may sound a bit strained, but the wise fool is ever a master of innuendo and one may read as much or as little into his sprightly sayings as he wishes. Certainly no deep, obscure meaning may be wrung out of Feste's allusion to Pythagoras and metempsychosis. Malvolio, however, does not seem aware that the mock-parson is calling him a fool, nor does he perceive the incongruity in a country parson's catechizing him on the beliefs of Pythagoras. The scene between the humiliated steward and his tormentor offers little more than good fooling and some further evidence of the upstart's willingness to trim his answers to all circumstances.

Feste does not take part in the scenes in which Maria and the others ensnare the pompous gull, and the reason that he does not is worth noting. Shakespeare seems to show us that a cruder kind of satire is needed to expose the folly of Malvolio than the wise fool is capable of administering. Feste's gay, ironical wit is exactly suited to commenting on the absurd extravagances of Orsino or Olivia. But a wily Maria and a buffoonish Sir Toby may properly exhibit Malvolio in all his ugly humour and make him aware of the foolish figure he cuts in the world's eye.

Shakespeare gives us another upstart in Parolles of *All's Well* and the fool Lavache to comment upon him. Parolles may have held a certain spurious attraction for Elizabethans, for, although he is a variant on the Latin *miles* and the Italian *capitano* and is finally exposed as a coward and a double-dealer, he is no windy braggart. Professor Krapp likens him to such soldier wits as George Pettie, Barnabie Riche, and Gascoigne, who helped to make Elizabethan English a bright and gaudy web of words.[33] But Parolles is, nevertheless, an upstart courtier and impostor; one who has gained credit as a sturdy soldier and friend chiefly by his shifty tongue and his gift of phrase. Not until late in the play does Bertram discover what a "damnable both-sides rogue" (*All's W.* IV, iii, 251) he is. Although Lavache takes no part in unmasking Parolles, he is quick to see through this "window of lattice" (II, iii, 225). The fool, according to his kind, phrases his contempt in witty language: "many a man's tongue shakes out his master's undoing. To say nothing, to do nothing, to know nothing, and to have nothing, is to be a great part of your title, which is within a very little of nothing" (II, iv, 24).

Himself a great talker, Lavache ridicules Parolles' love of smart language and persiflage.

PAR. . . . I am now, sir, muddied in Fortune's mood, and smell somewhat strong of her strong displeasure.
CLOWN. Truly, Fortune's displeasure is but sluttish if it smell so strongly as thou speak'st of. I will henceforth eat no fish of Fortune's butt'ring. Prithee allow the wind!
PAR. Nay, you need not to stop your nose, sir. I spake but by a metaphor.
CLOWN. Indeed, sir, if your metaphor stink, I will stop my nose, or against any man's metaphor. (V, ii, 4)[34]

Again it is the wise fool who playfully satirizes a less serious side of folly. Lavache leaves to others in the play the business of vigorously berating Parolles.

On the lighter side, the grotesque fopperies and glittering inanities of the puff gallant and the mushroom courtier provided a rich vein for the satirist or the ironical critic to work. The fashionable gentleman who has "undone three tailors" (*A.Y.L.* V, iv, 48) struts through many of the plays of this period. He appears in Jonson's distorting mirror as Fastidius Brisk and his feeble shadow Fungoso. But these gentlemen were no newcomers to the English stage.[35] Courtly Abusyon in Skelton's morality is no mere personified abstraction but a false, flattering courtier to King Henry VIII, who wears the frills and fopperies of his day.

COU. AB. Properly drest
All poynte deuys,
My persone prest
Beyonde all syse
Of the new gyse,
To russhe it oute
In euery route.
Beyond Measure
My sleue is wyde,
Al of Pleasure
My hose strayte tyde,
My buskyn wyde,
Ryche to beholde,
Gletterynge in golde.
(*Magnyfycence*, ll. 842–855)

In exposing the follies of this courtly pretender, the social satirist and the ironical commentator operate from widely differing motives and employ divergent methods. Impostors and affected asses are not really amusing to satirists like Jonson and Marston, if we may judge by their own pronouncements.[36] For these satirists, the body politic must be purged of the humours of social affectation if it is to be healthy, the strong emetic to be administered by a railing buffoon or an envious malcontent. To the ironical fool, on the other hand, such an attitude itself smacks of malicious folly. He has no wish to destroy his amusing puppets with derision. The most that he wants to do is to tickle their pomposities and watch them crow and dance on their strings. In a spirit of mock-courtesy, Lavache doffs his fool's cap to these beribboned gallants: "Faith, there's a dozen of 'em, with delicate fine hats, and most courteous feathers, which bow the head and nod at every man" (*All's W.* IV, v, 110). Without undue emphasis, Babulo laughs slyly at those silly fops who ransom their estates in order to go in gorgeous clothes: "follower I must cashere you: I must giue ouer houskeeping, tis the fashion, farewell boy" (*Patient Grissill*, III, l. 109).

In addition to wearing elegant clothes, the upstart gull affects huge and horrid oaths to fill the gaps in his imperfect speech. He would like to be thought witty or poetical and capable of a fine, taffeta phrase, but his speech usually stutters off into imbecility and monosyllables. Lavache mimicks just such a tongue-tied courtier who uses a single oath to suit all occasions:

COUNT. I pray you, sir, are you a courtier?
CLOWN. O Lord, sir! –There's a simple putting off. More, more! a hundred of them!
COUNT. Sir, I am a poor friend of yours, that loves you.
CLOWN. O Lord, sir! –Thick, thick, spare not me!
COUNT. I think, sir, you can eat none of this homely meat.
CLOWN. O Lord, sir! –Nay, put me to't, I warrant you.
COUNT. You were lately whipp'd, sir, as I think.
CLOWN. O Lord, sir! –Spare not me.
COUNT. Do you cry, 'O Lord, sir!' at your whipping, and 'Spare not me'? Indeed, your 'O Lord, sir!' is very sequent to your whipping. You would answer very well to a whipping, if you were but bound to't.
CLOWN. I ne'er had worse luck in my life in my 'O Lord, sir!' I see that things may serve long, but not serve ever. (*All's W.* II, ii, 40)[37]

Brandishing the two-edged blade of parody and direct satire, the clown Robin strikes at the affected speech and the expensive clothes of the knavish Sir Francis Ilf.

CLO. From Sir Iohn Harcop of Harcop, in the County of Yorke Knight, by me his man, to your selfe my young maister, by these presents greeting.
ILF. How camst thou by these good words?
CLOW. As you by your good cloaths, tooke them vpon trust, & swore I would neuer pay for em. (*Miseries*, sig. C2)

Sir Andrew Aguecheek, Shakespeare's most transparent gull, eagerly treasures up fragments of fustian cast off by others and tries to patch his awkward speech with them. It is probably Andrew's verbal infelicity that prompts Feste to mock him with the following gibberish:

CLOWN. I did impeticos thy gratillity; for Malvolio's nose is no whipstock. My lady has a white hand, and the Myrmidons are no bottle-ale houses.
AND. Excellent! Why, this is the best fooling, when all is done. (*Twel.* II, iii, 27)[38]

Unfortunately, Feste's encounters with Sir Andrew are few and brief. We might wish it were otherwise. But the chief part in gulling the foolish knight falls to the buffoon Sir Toby, who ungenerously pronounces Sir Andrew "a thin-fac'd knave, a gull" (V, i, 213) at the last. In a like manner, the feather-brained Emulo of *Patient Grissill* is exhibited and gulled not by Babulo but by the witty Lady Julia (III, ii, 9 ff.).

A happy device for showing forth the hollow vaunting but real timidity of the upstart is in the staged duel. The quarrel contrived between Sir Andrew and Viola-Cesario ends, of course, in fiasco, as does the similar duel between La-Foole and Daw in Jonson's *Epicoene* (IV, vi, 94). And the fantastic Emulo literally loses his spangled garters if not the cloth-of-gold hose attached thereby in his reported encounter with Sir Owen (*Patient Grissill,* III, ii, 51). But Passarello and Touchstone both undertake to prove by reverse logic the folly of these craven quarrellers. Passarello argues *ad absurdum* that a great quarreller is by definition "an arrant coward": "He that quarrels seekes to fight; and he that seekes to fight, seekes to dye; and he that seekes to dye, seekes never to fight more; and he that will quarrell and seekes meanes never to answer a man more, I thinke hees a coward" (*Malc.* V, i, 47).

Touchstone with this quarrel upon the seventh cause and his final evasion carries more conviction than does Passarello with his chop-logic. Possibly the reason is that Celia's fool buttresses his shaky argument with lively parody. With flashes of rapier wit, Touchstone pierces the absurd pretension of a code of courtly quarrelling.

TOUCH. I did dislike the cut of a certain courtier's beard. He sent me word, if I said his beard was not cut well, he was in the mind it was. This is call'd the Retort Courteous. If I sent him word again it was not well cut, he would send me word he cut it to please himself. This is call'd the Quip Modest. If again, it was not well cut, he disabled my judgment. This is call'd the Reply Churlish. If again, it was not well cut, he would answer I spake not true. This is call'd the Reproof Valiant. If again, it was not well cut, he would say I lie. This is call'd the Countercheck Quarrelsome; and so to the Lie Circumstantial and the Lie Direct.

JAQ. And how oft did you say his beard was not well cut?

TOUCH. I durst go no further than the Lie Circumstantial, nor he durst not give me the Lie Direct; and so we measur'd swords and parted. (*A.Y.L.* V, iv, 73)

Jaques chortles over Touchstone's grotesque wit but forgets that he himself had measured words with Orlando until the young lover gave him the "Reply Churlish" and drove him off (III, ii, 302).

Lavache suggests that the puff gallant peels off his gentility with his gloves: "Truly, madam, if God have lent a man any manners, he may easily put it off at court. He that cannot make a leg, put off's cap, kiss his hand, and say nothing, has neither leg, hands, lip, nor cap; and indeed such a fellow to say precisely, were not for the court . . ." (*All's W.* II, ii, 8). But it is Touchstone, again using self-parody, who epitomizes the folly of the courtly pretender: "I have trod a measure; I have flatt'red a lady; I have been politic with my friend, smooth with mine enemy; I have undone three tailors; I have had four quarrels, and like to have fought one" (*A.Y.L.* V, iv, 45).

Satire on Literary Affectations

A spirit of self-mockery and light, ironical humor is especially suited to satire on literary forms and fashions. One feels that Peele's *Old Wives' Tale* would have been immeasurably improved as parody had there been a motley fool lurking in the shadow of a great oak, waiting to guide us through the enchanted forest. One of the virtues of Shakespeare's *As You Like It* is that it has just such a wise fool.

Touchstone's gay, bantering tone is everywhere apparent. In narrating his whimsical wooing of Jane Smile, he lays bare all the delicious absurdity of the pastoral pretense: ". . . and I remember the wooing of a peascod instead of her, from whom I took two cods, and giving her them again, said with weeping tears, 'Wear these for my sake.' We that are true lovers run into strange capers . . ." (II, iv, 50). The impudent fool proves himself a clever parodist of both the style and substance of pastoral verse:

> If a hart do lack a hind,
> Let him seek out Rosalinde.
> If the cat will after kind,
> So be sure will Rosalinde.
> Winter garments must be lin'd,
> So must slender Rosalinde.
> They that reap must sheaf and bind,
> Then to cart with Rosalinde.
> Sweetest nut hath sourest rind,
> Such a nut is Rosalinde.
> He that sweetest rose will find
> Must find love's prick, and Rosalinde. (III, ii, 107)

In mocking the "false gallop" of Orlando's extravagant love lyrics, with their fourteener metre, Touchstone is also twitting the lovesick maiden whose wit has become infected with such inanities. It is small wonder that Rosalind dismisses him peevishly and quite inappropriately as a "dull fool" (III, ii, 121).

By gently reproving the folly of love in Rosalind and the other "country copulatives," Touchstone breathes an ironical spirit into an old satirical theme. Doting lovers and their foibles have been objects of ridicule ever since man grew to middle age and learned to smile at the absurdities of his youth. Erasmus' Moria claims for her own the fond lover who kisses the mole on his mistress's neck.[39] Plato's Socrates details the mad behavior of the infatuated lover in a half-mocking, half-serious manner (*Phaedrus* 251). The jesting Vice in John Heywood's *Play of Love* looks on the raptures and distractions of the lovers with amused contempt. Like Touchstone, Neither-Lover-Nor-Loved ridicules the ardent lovers by means of self-parody:

> Depper loue apparent in no twayne can be
> Quyte ouer the eares in loue and felt no ground
> Had not swymmyng holpe in loue I had ben dround
> But I swam by the shore vauntage to kepe
> To mock her in lone [loue] semyng to swym more depe. (583 ff.)

Heywood, of course, was not the first to bring the theme to the stage. A cynical amusement at the love affairs of his young master is the settled attitude of the wily slave of Plautus and Terence. Chrysalus, in *The Two Bacchides*, describes the chameleon mood of the lovesick Mnesilochus as follows:

> He's alive and well, if you have found his sweetheart;
> If not, he's ill and very like to die.
> His sweetheart is her lover's very soul;
> If she's away, he's nought; and if she's there,
> She makes his money nought, poor wretched fellow![40]

Almost the entire first scene of *Pseudolus* is given over to the slave's bantering of the heartstruck young Calidorus. Such jesting at the lover's humors probably descended to the *Commedia erudita* through Locatelli's adaptations of Latin comedy.[41] However, this form of mockery need not be explained as merely a dramatic convention. It is as old and as common as the comic spirit itself. When we come to the *Commedia dell'arte*, we witness a new approach to this age-old theme. In the coarser love affairs of the servants and zanni, we get a comic echo of the extravagant protestations, jealousies, and despairs of the principal lovers. In what seems to be the earliest pastoral scenario of Flaminio Scala, *L'Albore Incantato*, Arlecchino and Pedrolino provide comic relief by courting the nymphs until they are scared away by the thunder and flame of the magician.[42] Such parody offers a more subtle comment on the follies and humours of love than does direct disparagement. The device is also far more dramatic.

Shakespeare's indebtedness to Italian popular comedy, and especially to the pastoral romance, is rather generally accepted now.[43] To what extent he borrowed his plots and characters from Italian models is still a matter of conjecture. Certainly Shakespeare's use of an underplot as a comic echo of or contrast to the romantic intrigues of the main plot may have been a refinement upon earlier English models. The two servants who are suitors to the handmaid in Medwall's *Fulgens and Lucres* (c. 1497) present just such a parallel to the rival lovers of the main plot. But the particular affectation of love in a forest probably derives from Italian pastoral comedy. The earlier plays and playwrights differ markedly from Shakespeare in their manner of burlesquing pastoral love. The *burle*, like the briefer *lazzi*, of Italian comedy were usually extempore.[44] They were often crude and obscene. But, most important of all, these episodes were buffoonish in character. One laughs at the zanni's crude imitation of Flavio's love-making or sonneteering, but one laughs with Touchstone in his burlesque wooing of Audrey. The cream of the jest is that Touchstone knows exactly what he is about; he is the fully-conscious parodist.[45]

Another absurdity fostered in the pastoral tradition was the pose of rustic gentility and bucolic ease. Shepherds and shepherdesses disported themselves with all the elegance and grace of lords and ladies of the realm. Indeed, they often turned out to be gentlefolk masquerading in russet and frieze while on a rural holiday. The banished Duke who sets up his court in the Forest of Arden manages with his fellows to "fleet the time carelessly as they did in the golden world" (I, i, 124). But as he soberly contemplates the scene, he grows sententious: "Now, my co-mates and brothers in exile, / Hath not old custom made this life more sweet / Than that of painted pomp? Are not these woods / More free from peril than the envious court?" (II, i, 1). Such praise of the simple life of the country was, of course, traditional. Shakespeare might have found this theme in Chaucer, Sidney, Spenser, Drayton, Daniel, or Breton, or from among any number of his literary ancestors or contemporaries. A pastoral eclogue, novel, or play was hardly complete without some reflections upon country life and its superiority to town court life. Shakespeare's Henry VI had already hymned of these supposed advantages:

> Ah, what a life were this! how sweet! how lovely!
> Gives not the hawthorn bush a sweeter shade
> To shepherds looking on their silly sheep

> Than doth a rich embroider'd canopy
> To kings that fear their subjects' treachery?
> O yes, it doth! a thousandfold it doth!
> And to conclude, the shepherd's homely curds,
> His cold thin drink out of his leather bottle,
> His wonted sleep under a fresh tree's shade,
> All which secure and sweetly he enjoys,
> Is far beyond a prince's delicates,
> His viands sparkling in a golden cup,
> His body couched in a curious bed,
> When care, mistrust, and treason waits on him.
> (*3 H. VI* II, v, 41)

Amiens' Song reiterates the same theme, though in lovelier language.

The sentiment has a certain quaint appeal for most of us, particularly after we have been hurt or wearied by the world of men. But it charms not that prudent humorist Touchstone. With sturdy common sense, he observes: "Ay, now am I in Arden, the more fool I! When I was at home, I was in a better place; but travellers must be content" (II, iv, 16). When put to the question by Corin, the fool delivers a mock-encomium on the shepherd's life: "Truly, shepherd, in respect of itself, it is a good life; but in respect that it is a shepherd's life, it is naught. In respect that it is solitary, I like it very well; but in respect that it is private, it is a vile life. Now in respect it is in the fields, it pleaseth me well; but in respect it is not in the court, it is tedious. As it is a spare life, look you, it fits my humour well; but as there is no more plenty in it, it goes much against my stomach" (III, ii, 13).[46] To see the sprightly fool capering about in the stately vestments of euphuism is ludicrous indeed. Through his whimsical parody, Touchstone further inflates the turgid phrase, the ornamental diction, and the exaggerated sentiments of arcadian romance until, like a shimmering soap bubble, it bursts amidst a cascade of good-natured laughter.

Few other fools in the plays of Shakespeare or his contemporaries function so consistently as literary critics. Will Summers makes some random, not very pointed references to a currently popular Spanish romance translated into English as *The Mirror of Knighthood* and to its grandiloquent hero Donzel del Phebo or the Knight of the Sun.[47] But it is Beaumont who fully burlesques this kind of writing through Ralph of *The Knight of the Burning Pestle* (c. 1607). Babulo, the clever clown of Haughton, Chettle, and Dekker's *Patient Grissill*, has some fun with the prevailing craze for fantastic travelogues at the same time that he ridicules the pretentious scholar Laureo:

BA. . . . you stand all day peeping into an ambrie there, and talke of monsters and miracles, and countries to no purpose: before I fell to my trade I was a traueller, and found more in one yeare then you can by your poets and paltries in seauen yeares.

LAU. What wonders hast thou seene, which are not heere?

BA. O God, I pittie thy capacitye good scholler: as a little wind makes a sweet ball smell, so a crumme of learning makes your trade proude: what wonders? wonders not of nine daies, but 1599. I haue seene vnder *Iohn Prester* and *Tamer Cams*, people with heds like Dogs. (V, i, 10)

And Passarello quotes a few lines from *Orlando Furioso* in mocking Maquerelle (*Malc.* V, ii, 41). But such brief and casual references do not add up to literary parody or criticism. Touchstone alone among the fools in these plays combines in his ironical remarks a criticism of the social and the literary affectations of his day.[48]

The Witty Fool versus the Foolish Wit

When Duke Senior observes of Touchstone that "He uses his folly like a stalking horse, and under the presentation of that he shoots his wit" (*A.Y.L.* V, iv, 111), he is defining for us the ironical pose of the wise fool. Critics have justly applied this description to others of Shakespeare's fools as well. But to get at the full pith of this ripe observation, we must not pluck it from the context in which it grows and has its meaning. Jaques has just been exhibiting his "motley-minded gentleman" (V, iv, 41) for the Duke's approval. Touchstone has cut some capers and delivered a travesty on the courtly manner of quarreling. This bit of burlesque satire delights his audience, while playing up to their smug sense of superiority. The Duke appreciates the manner as well as the matter of the satire. Touchstone's technique is deft by comparison with the bludgeoning strokes of Jaques' invective.

Doubtless Duke Senior would have approved of Dryden's definition: "the nicest and most delicate touches of satire consist in fine raillery. . . . How easy it is to call rogue and villain, and that wittily! But how hard to make a man appear a fool, a blockhead, or a knave, without using any of those opprobrious terms. . . . There is still a vast difference betwixt the slovenly butchering of a man, and the fineness of a stroke that separates the head from the body, and leaves it standing in its place."[49] Here the two methods of satirically attacking a subject or a person are sharply contrasted. The railing buffoon and the malcontent satirist hack away at their victims with a cleaver; the wise, ironical fool parries and thrusts with his rapierlike wit. It would be tempting to vary Dryden's metaphor and say that the victim of the wise fool's stabbing wit may bleed internally without knowing that he has been hurt. But the truth is that no one suffers seriously from the strokes of the fool's satire. Sometimes the gulls and impostors are made a little uncomfortable by the stinging pricks or bird-bolts, but their skins are thick and impervious to such fine criticism. For the most part, these creatures are unaware that they have been attacked or made sport of.

To avoid further generalizing, let us return to the play that exhibits both an ironical and a crudely satirical commentator. In *As You Like It*, the melancholy Jaques, railing upon his mistress the world, is set in nice contrast to the laughing philosopher Touchstone. Both characters, be it noted, are Shakespeare's additions to Lodge's ensemble of shepherds and foresters. Jaques' has been a popular though misunderstood role on the stage from the first. Just as he succeeds in calling fools into a circle by pronouncing the mystic word "ducdame" three times (II, v, 56), so Jaques has managed to impose upon his audience in some measure by pronouncing other, more magical words of his master. John Palmer is probably right in saying that Shakespeare intends us to take the melancholy gentleman somewhat at his own valuation.[50] To have shown us Jaques crowing like chanticleer but missing the whole point of the fool's jest would have exposed him too completely at the outset.

However, it is a very literal-minded reader or playgoer, indeed, who accepts Jaques wholly at his own valuation. To see a parallel between Touchstone and Jaques on the one hand and Passarello and Malevole on the other is to miss the heart of Shakespeare's comic situation. Passarello echoes the bitter and scurrilous railing of Malevole, though in a less somber key.

MAL. And how dooth thy olde Lord that hath wit enough to be a flatterer, and conscience enough to be a knave?

PASSAR. O excellent, he keepes beside me fifteen jeasters, to instruct him in the Art of fooling, and utters their jeastes in private to the Duke and Dutchesse; hele be like to your Switzer, or Lawyer; heele be of any side for most mony. (*Malc.* I, vii, 132)

As Professor Stoll remarks, Malevole draws Passarello out, to "revel in his grotesque wisdom, and eagerly fling it in the face of the more foolish world."[51] But is it true that Touchstone plays a like subordinate role to Jaques? Malevole and Passarello might almost have changed places, but Jaques and Touchstone could hardly have done the like. The melancholy man delights in the fool's grotesque wit, but he does not really comprehend it. Although Jaques says that he is "ambitious for a motley coat" (*A.Y.L.* II, vii, 43), he would have worn it with a very bad grace. The bells would have jangled horribly out of tune had he tried to put on Touchstone's cap, for he lacks the gay, whimsical spirit which animates the wise fool.

Jaques' misanthropy and scurrilous satire, which provoke the Duke to a scornful tirade, only excite mirth in Touchstone and incline him to parody. By roundly rebuking the old shepherd Corin, the ironical fool makes his sly comment on Jaques, Chapman's Dowsecer,[52] and all other malcontents out of love with life and the reproductive process: "That is another simple sin in you: to bring the ewes and the rams together and to offer to get your living by the copulation of cattle; to be bawd to a bell-wether, and to betray a she-lamb of a twelvemonth to a crooked-pated old cuckoldly ram, out of all reasonable match. If thou beest not damn'd for this, the devil himself will have no shepherds; I cannot see else how thou shouldst scape" (III, ii, 82).

Catching a hint from the Duke's accusation and Jaques' defense of himself, several critics have discovered a lampoon on a contemporary satirist. G. B. Harrison tries to link Jaques' name and person to Sir John Harington, translator of Ariosto and author of *The Metamorphosis of Ajax* (1596).[53] Arthur Gray is certain that it is through Jaques that Shakespeare administered his reported "purge" of Ben Jonson.[54] Marston also becomes a logical candidate for butt of Shakespeare's ridicule. Even the pompous language of one of Marston's early satirical poems suggests Jaques' metaphor: "Now, Satyre cease to rub our gauled skinnes, / And to unmaske the worlds detested sinnes. / Thou shalt as soone draw *Nilus* riuer dry, / As clense the world from foule impietie."[55] Professor Campbell is probably right in asserting that "Jaques is thus no unfriendly portrait of any one satirist of the time," but that Shakespeare glances through him at several of the formal and dramatic satirists and rejects the tone of their writings as too severe and presumptuous.[56]

Lest any of his auditors should miss the high comedy or the glancing satire in Jaques' role, Shakespeare furnishes several commentators to underscore his intention. Again it is Touchstone who best fulfills this function. He reduces to burlesque or raises to hyperbole all of the latent absurdity in Jaques' pose. With a mock show of violence, the fool berates the contented shepherd Corin: "Most shallow man! Thou worm's meat in respect of a good piece of flesh indeed! Learn of the wise, and perpend. Civet is of a baser birth than tar—the very uncleanly flux of a cat" (III, ii, 67). At one stroke he hits off the morbid spirit and the mordant tone of Jaques' invective—and of Marston's. The victim of his bantering humor is not always present when Touchstone laughs at him. In his mock-eulogy on the pastoral life, the fool again addresses Corin the shepherd, but he is also thinking of the malcontent philosopher Jaques. The sentimental cynic grieving over the stricken deer is not at hand to hear the gay fool lamenting over the poor lamb betrayed to the cuckoldly old ram, but he is in our thoughts. Touchstone enjoys ridiculing folly for his own amusement.

Apparently unaware of his audience, the fool in the forest makes genial fun of Jaques' tiresome moralizing when he draws forth his timepiece and solemnly descants upon the passage of time:

> 'It is ten o'clock.
> Thus we may see,' quoth he, 'how the world wags.
> 'Tis but an hour ago since it was nine,
> And after one hour more 'twill be eleven;
> And so, from hour to hour, we ripe and ripe,
> And then, from hour to hour, we rot and rot. . . .'
> (II, vii, 22)

Meanwhile, Jaques looks on patronizingly and laughs at what should embarrass him. His imperturbable self-esteem makes Jaques ludicrous to others but never to himself. The bird-bolts of Touchstone's parody ricochet harmlessly from him and tickle rather than irritate his vast complacency. While eavesdropping on Touchstone and Audrey in the third act, Jaques smugly comments: "O knowledge ill-inhabited, worse than Jove in a thatch'd house!" (III, iii, 10). But two acts later when Touchstone describes Audrey: "Rich honesty dwells like a miser, sir, in a poor house, as your pearl in your foul oyster" (V, iv, 62), the sententious Jaques misses the relevance of this remark.

To the ironical fool, it does not greatly matter whether or not his comments and mimicry are overheard and seen, since he has no real desire to purge or reform anyone. He likes his simpering gallants well enough as they are. The wise fool will not lift his finger or his voice to drive the swaggering courtier or the pretentious pedant from the stage, but he certainly will laugh at his folly and his presumption. Touchstone, Will Summers, and Feste all assume the traditional attitude of the ironical man. Like Dicaeopolis and the buffoon of the Dorian mime, they smile expectantly, knowing that the strutting impostor sooner or later will stumble over his own false conceits.[57] Sometimes the Greek εἴρων would help his victim along with encouraging words or a well-timed nudge, but the characteristic attitude of the wise fool is one of detached amusement. He leaves the role of victimizer to the Marias and Brainworms of the play.

Touchstone, the parodist, also differs from the railing Jaques in his attitude toward himself. In keeping with the conventional behavior of the ironical man, Touchstone constantly depreciates himself. We have already noted in his reply to Rosalind how he pretends to less conscious wisdom than he possesses: "Nay I shall ne'er be ware of mine own wit till I break my shins against it" (II, iv, 59). It is also part of his ironical pose to concede as much cleverness to the clown William as he grants himself: "By my troth, we that have good wits have much to answer for; we shall be flouting; we cannot hold" (V, i, 12). No astute person will be entirely taken in by the fool's protestations of modesty. Yet his modesty is not altogether an affectation, for in all true parody there is ever present a spirit of self-mockery that leavens the criticism and prevents it from becoming merely censorious.

It is altogether appropriate that the foolish wit should be opposed by the witty fool; that the solemn Jaques be laughed at by the ironical Touchstone. If Jaques, with his febrile satire and his cynical posturing, is Shakespeare's transmutation of a traditional type of learned fraud, Touchstone is no less a metamorphosed being. He is far closer to Erasmus' Moria than he is to Marcolf or Cacurgus. The Touchstone who parodies, at times even travesties, the pastoral tradition is an agent of gentle literary satire. But the critic who sees through the charming sham and yet gaily puts on the manners of Arcadia is essentially an ironical person. "By their fruits ye shall know them" (Matt. vii, 16). The seeds of criticism that the scornful buffoon and the malcontent satirist scatter abroad ripen into cynicism and sour pessimism; the wise fool's comments grow into comical and genial tolerance of human weakness.

Chapter VI. THE FOOL IN THE FABLE

IN LOOKING TOO HARD and long at the fools in the plays of Shakespeare and his contemporaries, we may easily lose our sense of perspective. Insensibly we may allow our focus to become so distorted that the fool emerges as the epitome of all that is comic, pathetic, or tragic in the several plays in which he appears. If this study were to have that effect, it would tend to warp and diminish, not enlarge, our understanding of Shakespeare and his fellow dramatists.

We are not likely to exaggerate the importance of Marston's or Middleton's fools—fools who are readily separable from their plays. Whether or not Passarello was Marston's later addition to *The Malcontent* we cannot certainly say,[1] but his part could easily have been added. He is not essential to the play's plot or meaning. His comments are but muffled and buffoonish echoes of Malevole's railings, and they are too general or too incidental to reflect much upon the characters or the meaning of the action. This fool lacks the moral and ironical detachment that would fit him to serve as a comic chorus. What is true of Passarello is almost equally true of Dondolo, Marston's other fool, and of Middleton's Pickadill. Pickadill is only a little more ironical in his comments than are Passarello and Dondolo. As a witty, satirical commentator, he differs very little from the wily servant Savourwit, in *No Wit, No Help Like a Woman's*. Middleton might have dispensed with Pickadill without greatly altering the character of his comedy. None of these three fools has a spark of human sympathy large enough to warm an old lecher's heart or a young lady's vanity. Criticism has probably given them their due by wholly ignoring them.

Will Summers, however, does lend himself to the kind of focal distortion that we have just mentioned. The fool plays an unduly prominent part in Rowley's chronicle history play. He is the constant companion of King Henry VIII except for a brief episode in which Henry travels about London incognito, and he speaks more lines than does any other character but the King.[2] The very weight and force of his speeches make him more than a match for Cardinal Wolsey—the arch-intriguer of this Protestant tract. Rowley's *When You See Me, You Know Me* would certainly have offended the taste of earlier writers on dramatic decorum. One would almost think that George Whetstone had seen Rowley's Will Summers when he wrote: "Manye tymes (to make mirthe) they make a Clowne companion with a Kinge: in theyr graue Counsels, they allow the aduise of fooles . . ."[3] Plays similar to Rowley's incurred the august displeasure of Sir Philip Sidney and prompted him to comment: "all theyr Playes be neither right Tragedies, nor right Comedies; mingling Kings and Clownes, not because the matter so carrieth it, but thrust in Clownes by head and shoulders, to play a part in maiesticall matters, with neither decencie nor discretion . . ."[4]

Whoever wrote the Prologue to the Shakespearean *King Henry the Eighth* may well have been thinking of Rowley's chronicle history play when he advised his audience:

> Only they
> That come to hear a merry bawdy play,
> A noise of targets, or to see a fellow
> In a long motley coat guarded with yellow
> Will be deceiv'd. For, gentle hearers, know,
> To rank our chosen truth with such a show
> As fool and fight is, besides forfeiting
> Our own brains and the opinion that we bring
> To make that only true we now intend,
> Will leave us never an understanding friend.
> (Prologue, ll. 13–22)

Of course, Rowley had other fish to fry than pilchards or true Kingfish when he wrote his merry, bawdy play of Henry VIII. He was interested in slanting history in such a way as to throw Wolsey into the worst possible light. And for his satirical purposes, the witty Will Summers of tradition served admirably. Viewed from this angle, the fool's presence and prominence do not altogether destroy the dramatic verisimilitude of the play.

The Fool in the Tragic Fable

The question of artistic propriety comes up again when we consider the role of the Fool in *King Lear*. Does Shakespeare violate the canon of decorum or seemliness when he introduces the Fool as companion to the King? Sidney, who took the classical stricture against mingling tragical and comical figures in the same play rather literally,[5] would probably have disapproved of Shakespeare's tragedy as a dramatic mélange. But would he have been warranted in thus condemning *King Lear*—even by renaissance critical standards? Can it truly be said that Shakespeare thrusts the Fool in "by head and shoulders, to play a part in maiesticall matters"? The Fool may sleep with the spaniels or dine with the scullery wench, but he spends most of his waking hours in the company of the King. He belongs at court by right of office. And since the court is where the king is, the Fool is always at home whether in Lear's palace or in a hovel on the heath. But if the fool belongs traditionally beside his master, does he necessarily belong in this play? We may dismiss as irrelevant the fact that this late Elizabethan fool is something of an anachronism in the old legend of Leir. The important question remains: Is the fool's presence consonant with the high, serious tone of tragedy? Should Shakespeare have allowed the conventionally carefree fool to follow his master out on the stormy heath? In his feeble attempts to outjest the elements and the fiercer storm in Lear's brain, does the Fool not become a little ridiculous? Are his characteristic speech and behavior too trifling for so somber a tragedy? To answer these and other questions, we need to inquire a little further into the doctrine of artistic decorum.

George Puttenham, in discussing decency of speech and behavior, observes that: "the thing that may well become one man to do may not become another, and that which is seemely to be done in this place is not so seemely in that, and at such a time decent, but at another time vndecent . . ."[6] Critics since the time of Horace[7] have insisted upon the poet's responsibility to make his characters speak and behave in a typical or at least a consistent manner. Richard Edwards, in the Prologue to his *Damon and Pithias* (1571), puts it quaintly:

In comedies the greatest skill is this: rightly to touch
All things to the quick, and eke to frame each person so
That by his common talk you may his nature rightly know
A roister ought not preach—that were too strange to hear,—
But, as from virtue he doth swerve, so ought his words appear.
The old man is sober; the young man rash; the lover triumphing in joys;
The matron grave; the harlot wild, and full of wanton toys:
Which all in one course they no wise so agree,
So correspondent to their kind their speeches ought to be. (ll. 14–22)[8]

Of course, no modern critic would apply so arbitrary a rule in measuring a character of Shakespeare's. Shakespeare seldom cast his characters strictly according to type. He had the rarer skill to make the roistering Sir John Falstaff preach in the manner of Euphues and yet remain a credible rogue. His Hamlet is no typical blood-avenger, nor his Fool in *Lear* a boisterous clown. But not even Shakespeare could wholly disregard popular and traditional conceptions that had grown up around certain character types. Since the fool traditionally was lighthearted and nimble-witted, Lear's Fool could be no less. Shakespeare was thus confronted by a twofold problem. He must make his Fool talk, sing, and tumble like a fool and at the same time set him moving in a tragic situation. For the rules of decorum require not only that a character behave in a manner consistent with himself but that he speak and act in a fashion suitable to the occasion.[9] Upon his transplanting to the tragic heath, the Fool must not appear to be an exotic growth but a thoroughly indigenous part of the landscape.

Tragedy, like comedy, has its characteristic tone or ethos. Scaliger, who echoes Aristotle's definition with some slight variation, finds that tragedy differs from comedy chiefly in the nature of the action and the persons represented and in the kind of language employed. "Tragedy . . . employs kings and princes, whose affairs are those of the city, the fortress, and the camp. A tragedy opens more tranquilly than a comedy, but the outcome is horrifying. The language is grave, polished, removed from the colloquial."[10] The Fool, of course, speaks a colloquial language. His proverbs and scraps of old songs are of popular origin and would certainly fit Puttenham's description of the base or humble style (Bk. III, Ch. vi). The fact that he sometimes quotes doggerel rhymes would seem further to disqualify his speech for tragic utterance. How then are we to reconcile the Fool's lowly, unrhetorical talk to the lofty, heroical temper of this tragedy? We ought to grant at the outset that this disparity between style and substance is wide and cannot be bridged satisfactorily by traditional standards. In *King Lear*, Shakespeare does not adhere to the letter or forms of decorum, but he does preserve the sense of decorum in the King-Fool scenes. The Fool does not violate our sense of dramatic propriety by what he says or what he does.

Something further may be said to extenuate the colloquial nature of the Fool's speech. The plainness and artless simplicity, aspects of the humble style,[11] are at times quite proper to the mood of an elemental tragedy like *Lear*. When threatened with the whip, the Fool replies with a disabling figure: "Truth's a dog must to kennel; he must be whipp'd out, when Lady the brach may stand by th' fire and stink" (*Lear* I, iv, 124).[12] There is a world of tragic meaning in the simple comment of the Fool when he learns that Regan too has turned ingrate: "Winter's not gone yet, if the wild geese fly that way" (II, iv, 46).[13] Obviously the Fool's speech is not really artless. When he hides his meaning in metaphor or uses the tags from old songs as covert allusions to Goneril's unkindness or Lear's unwisdom, he is merely practising the art that conceals art. The Fool is essentially a poet when he compresses the tragic meaning of old Gloucester's life into a few lines: "Now a little fire in a wild field were like an old lecher's heart—a small spark, all the rest on's body cold"

(III, iv, 116). Surely such an utterance does not detract from the tragic solemnity of the play.

Not only in his style of speaking but in his other behavior as well, the character in tragedy was supposed to bear himself in the grand manner. Even madness and villainy are represented in *Lear* on a heroic scale. Should not the Fool be expected to conform in his way to this scale? In answering this question, we must be on our guard to avoid that distorted focus which sees the Fool as the central figure in the play, next to Lear himself. He is not, nor was he meant to be; otherwise Shakespeare would never have discarded him midway through the play. It is not even certain that he is the focal center of one of the play's important ideas—the wisdom of seeming folly. Edgar, although he wears no motley, probably comes as close as the Fool does to Erasmus' conception of the wise fool—one of those simple souls with whom God peoples the Kingdom of Heaven. This Fool, like all other professional fools, is normally a gay, whimsical entertainer whose duty it is to jest his master out of his black moods. That he fails and is swept off the stage only reminds us that we are witnessing tragedy. This frail figure of a man stumbling out on the heath with the storm shrieking overhead is pathetic indeed. He may strike some spectators as absurdly grotesque in his tattered motley, but he is no more ridiculous in himself than is a crippled child or a fragile old man. Even though the Fool is drawn into tragedy somewhat against his will and his own good sense, he accepts the role thrust upon him. And in playing this role, the Fool approaches the heroic. His patience, at least, is monumental.

How then does Shakespeare manage to fit motley into the buskin? For there is no doubt that the Fool does acquire something of the stature of a tragic figure. Not just any fool would have served Shakespeare's turn. Will Summers would have been too self-satisfied, and Lavache would have been too self-indulgent. We cannot even agree with Austin Gray that Lear's Fool is merely "Feste astray in a world of tragedy,"[14] though these two fools are akin to one another. What Feste would have been like in a tragic setting is idle to conjecture. Certainly Lear's Fool is affected by the tragic circumstances as much or more than he affects them. There is no question but that Lear and his play would be poorer without the Fool. The examples of Nahum Tate's version (1681) and of the several eighteenth century productions of *Lear* present clear evidence of what happens when the play is tampered with and the Fool's role is omitted.

D. Nichol Smith is probably right when he remarks that: "the artful prattle of the Fool does more than give variety and relax the strain on one's feelings. It makes Lear's lot endurable to us, but at the same time gives us a keener sense of its sadness. . . . In a word, the Fool intensifies the pathos by relieving it."[15] It need not surprise us that Professor Smith resorts to paradox to describe the dramatic function of the Fool in *Lear*. The Fool, by his very nature, invites such a critical approach. He is compounded of a number of opposite qualities. Like most wise fools, he disguises his wit in the garb of folly. He is sometimes grave and sometimes gay, like Horace's prodigy (*Satires* I, x, 11), but he often merges both moods in the same song or jest. This mixture of jest with earnest lifts his pun out of banality: "thou shalt have as many dolours for thy daughters as thou canst tell in a year" (*Lear* II, iv, 54). He would have answered well to Cicero's description of the solemn, ironical jester.[16] He is both the sweet and bitter fool of his own song, for behind his sharpest taunts there moves a tender love for Lear.

LEAR. When were you wont to be so full of songs, sirrah?
FOOL. I have us'd it, nuncle, ever since thou mad'st thy daughters thy mother; for when thou gav'st them the rod, and put'st down thine own breeches,
[Sings] Then they for sudden joy did weep,
And I for sorrow sung,
That such a king should play bo-peep
And go the fools among. (I, iv, 185)

The Fool combines a shrewd knowledge of the ways of this world with a more than earthly wisdom. When things go from bad to worse with Lear, he laments: "Fortune, that arrant whore, / Ne'er turns the key to th' poor" (II, iv, 52). But when that worse grows even worse, the Fool sings with stoic resignation:

He that has and a little tiny wit—
With hey, ho, the wind and the rain—
Must make content with his fortunes fit,
For the rain it raineth every day. (III, ii, 74)

Only a complex personality could hold such contrarieties in equipoise. The Fool functions as something of a mediator in *Lear*. Although he does not weaken the play as tragedy, he does soften its austerity and humanize it for us.

The Fool in the Comic Fable

As Lear's Fool stands between us and the full force of tragedy, Feste stands in a like relation to comedy. The fool does not lessen our laughter at the antics and inanities of the Illyrians. On the contrary, he brightens the comedy by making it gayer and more graceful. His songs charm us and his witty sallies tease us into thoughtful laughter. In moving upstairs and below stairs in the Lady Olivia's household, Feste the fool acts as a link between the romantic main plot and the farcical underplot. It would be absurd to say that without Feste *Twelfth Night* would fall apart. The fool is not that important to the play's structure. But it is certainly true that without Feste *Twelfth Night* would be a different and far less satisfying comedy. The delightful romance might easily slip into melodrama and the brittle comedy of humors sink into mere farce without the subtle comic sense that Feste brings with him into the play.[17]

What is there in Feste's character that ideally fits him for the role of comic mediator? First of all, he takes a detached and ironical view of everyone and everything about him. His perception of the incongruous and of the relativity of things is pervasive and complete. No other fool would have remarked: "Nothing that is so is so" (*Twel.* IV, i, 9). Later, in a passage larded with nonsense, Feste returns to this theme: "as the old hermit of Prague, that never saw pen and ink, very wittily said to a niece of King Gorboduc, 'That that is is'; so I, being Master Parson, am Master Parson; for what is 'that' but that, and 'is' but is?" (IV, ii, 14). But if he seems to be contradicting his earlier statement and arguing now for the validity of appearances, this impression too is deceptive. The fool has just been putting on the gown of a cleric, which becomes him, he says, as "an honest man and a good housekeeper" rather better than as "a careful man and a great scholar" (IV, ii, 10). There is a sort of redoubling irony in all this, since Feste is none of these persons. The very act of putting on the parson's gown is for Feste an exercise in irony, since the disguise was not necessary to the gulling of Malvolio in a darkened cell.

But if we feel the ground beginning to shift a little under our feet, we need not be alarmed, for to Feste the recognition that appearance and reality are not always one is no occasion for bitterness or metaphysical pessimism. Such a recognition adds a tang and sometimes even a pensive touch to his foolery, but nothing more.[18] Feste is no precursor to the romantic ironists of the nineteenth century. His irony is no *transzendentale Buffonerie*,[19] nor is there any of that cosmic indifference in it such as prompts Gloucester to rail: "As flies to wanton boys are we to th' gods. / They kill us for their sport" (*Lear* IV, i, 36). Feste's ironical perception is no excuse for amorality as it is for certain modern Gloucesters. His attitude is traditional; one which he shares with Socrates, Erasmus, and most humanists. His recognition that truth often belies appearances leads Feste not away from but toward a comic and a moral view of life.

And so we come to a second and equally important aspect of Feste's comic role. The fool serves not only as an ironical commentator but also as a moral touchstone to the play. Paradoxical as this statement may seem, the irresponsible fool is really a moral being. No comedy deserving the name can live long that is without some system of accepted values. If Pickadill and Passarello fall short of being comic spokesmen, the fault lies in the fact that both these fools and their plays lack any recognizable moral system. Shakespeare, however much he may have played dramatically with moral ideas, does not make the mistake of leaving them out of his plays.

What then is the moral or ethical system underlying *Twelfth Night*, which finds expression or embodiment in Feste and Viola?[20] If we say that it is essentially Aristotelian, we do not mean to suggest that Shakespeare was a scholar or a schoolman. He need not have read Aristotle in the Greek or Aquinas in the Latin to have come by these ideas.[21] Concepts of temperance and the golden mean were not only in the air and on everybody's lips; they were also to be found in the grammar school textbooks in rhetoric. With Terence as a model and with the vast commentary on his plays as guides, the schoolboy learned the ethical precepts of Aristotle by proxy.[22] Terence, of course, served as a storehouse of moral epigrams, but it was believed that he taught by example as well as by precept. A recent critic, Marvin Herrick, claims that Terence illustrates Aristotelian principles in his play *Adelphi.* In the course of this play, says Herrick, the niggardly Demea and the prodigal Micio temper their vices and approach each other in the mean of liberality.[23] How then does Aristotle's *Ethics* relate to Feste and the play of *Twelfth Night*? Certainly the fool is not simply a mouthpiece for ethical maxims; he is not so sententious as is Touchstone. Feste does not spout ethics, but he lives according to the golden mean in this joyous comedy. As we have suggested earlier, he moderates between the sentimentality of the high comedy and the heartlessness of the low comedy.

The first and most obvious way in which Feste illustrates the principle of moderation is in his jesting. Although he wears motley, this professional fool well fits Wilson's description of the pleasant wiseman: "the consideration of time, and moderation of pastime, and seldome vsing of drie mockes, euen when neede most requireth, make a difference, and shew a seuerall vnderstanding betwixt a common iester, and a pleasaunt wiseman."[24] Though the language in which it is phrased is Elizabethan, Wilson's distinction between the common or alehouse jester and the pleasant wiseman goes back to Cicero (*De Oratore* II, lx, 247), who in turn derives it from Aristotle (*Nic. Eth.* II, vii, 13 [1108a]). Wilson's pleasant wiseman closely corresponds to Aristotle's man of wit (εὐτράπελος), who observes a mean between the extremes of the buffoon (βωμολόχος), who must have his jest at all costs, and the boor (ἀγροῖκος), who completely lacks a sense of humor. At another place (*Rhet.* III, xviii, 7 [1419b]), Aristotle speaks of irony rather than buffoonery as the kind of wit befitting a gentleman. Evidence that Shakespeare knew and approved of Aristotelian and Ciceronian attitudes toward jesting comes from an early comedy. In *Love's Labour's Lost,* Rosaline commends Berowne as "a merrier man, / Within the limit of becoming mirth, / I never spent an hour's talk withal" (II, i, 66). The fulsome Sir Nathaniel, from the same play, shows a like appreciation for pleasant wit: "Your reasons at dinner have been sharp and sententious; pleasant without scurrility, witty without affection, audacious without impudency, learned without opinion, and strange without heresy" (*L.L.L.* V, i, 2). This description of the pedantical bore Holofernes would much better become the urbane Feste.

Feste's audacity in calling his mistress fool and in proving the charge comes very close to impudence. What saves him is his wit and the truth in his rebuke. Olivia has the good grace to admit the propriety of the fool's reproof: "What think you of this fool, Malvolio? Doth he not mend?" (*Twel.* I, v, 79). Of course, Malvolio, who through his self-love lacks a sense of humor and proportion, sees only the impertinence and not the ironical wit of the fool. But if Feste's good-humored fooling contrasts with Malvolio's total lack of wit; it also contrasts with the buffoonish extravagances of Sir Toby and the pretty malice of the intriguing Maria. The fool observes a mean in jesting, between buffoonery and boorishness. He has wit enough to laugh at absurdity, but he was the greater wit to know when and how much to laugh. In the practice of his merry profession, Feste keeps an artful decorum. As Viola remarks of him, "He must observe their mood on whom he jests, / The quality of persons, and the time; / Not, like the haggard, check at every feather / That comes before his eye" (III, i, 69). Feste, no doubt, looks archly at Sir Toby as he commends the fat knight for his "admirable fooling" (II, iii, 85). He needs not the inspiration of Momus or Bacchus to put him into good fooling.

The fool, at one time or another, passes upon most of the persons in the play, but he varies his manner with the mood and quality of the person on whom he jests. He delights the silly Sir Andrew with gibberish and apparent nonsense. Sir Toby revels in the fool's exquisite mockery of Malvolio in the darkened cell. Feste exchanges parry for thrust with the wily Maria. And, as we have just noted, he skirts the edge of impudence with his mistress Olivia. He plays up to the Duke's affected melancholy with a dolorous song and then skips off with an ambiguous compliment. Later, when the Duke is in a happier mood, Feste appeals to Orsino's sententious spirit with a fantastic paradox. To Viola, who loves language so well that she sometimes abuses it, Feste appears first as a "corrupter of words." But, though he enjoys punning as much as Viola does, the fool is aware of the treachery in words: "A sentence is but a chev'ril glove to a good wit. How quickly the wrong side may be turn'd outward" (III, i, 12). There seems to be some understanding between these two.[25] Viola shows by her comments that she justly appreciates the wisdom of the fool.

Feste keeps a measure even in his mocking of Malvolio. He is the first to relent and provide the hoodwinked steward with paper, ink, and a light with which to win his release. It ought to be remembered that Feste, although he confesses to a part in the intrigue, actually is not present at the baiting of the yellow-stockinged, cross-gartered gull. Instead, his role as ironical commentator is taken by the less subtle Fabian. Feste is for other and more dancing measures. His mind is as supple and agile as ever his body was. He wears his Latinity and his learning as jauntily as his cap and bells. The fool is as far from Maria and Sir Toby in the tenor of his jesting as high comedy is from low. While they bang heavily at one end of the scale, Feste trips lightly over the keys with a gay and glancing wit.

As a representative of merry, old England, the fool stands obstinately against the new dispensation in the shape of the upstart Malvolio. When Sir Toby taunts the self-righteous steward, "Dost thou think because thou art virtuous, there shall be no more cakes and ale?" Feste chimes in, "Yes, by Saint Anne! And ginger shall be hot i' th' mouth too" (II, iii, 123). But though he identifies himself with the conservative party—the party of music and graceful manners, Feste is nothing allied to Sir Toby's drunkenness. He makes his position clear when Sir Toby staggers on to the stage in Act One. In answer to Olivia's query, "What's a drunken man like, fool?" Feste replies with a threefold simile: "Like a drown'd man, a fool, and a madman. One draught above heat makes him a fool, the second mads him, and a third drowns him" (I, v, 138). Although he is probably no model of temperance, Feste is no drunken sot either. Shakespeare never brings him on the stage in the reeling state in which Passarello and Pickadill sometimes appear. He would not have been in his proper character as the wise fool.

Feste takes a pivotal relation to some other ideas and emotions in the play. *Twelfth Night* is not just another comedy with a romantic plot; it is a comedy on the varieties and distortions of love. As Eric Bentley observes, "The romance shows love on the higher plane, the comedy of

Sir Toby love on a lower plane. On either plane love may be true or false, genuine or spurious."[26] The fool does not exhibit in himself any of the several kinds or degrees of love. He is almost the only character who does not appear at one time or another in the role of lover, and for this reason he, like Neither-Lover-Nor-Loved in Heywood's *Play of Love*, may well serve as the ironical bystander. Viola belongs to the very heart of the play. She is central to the romantic plot and to the varying conceptions of love. Her genuine, selfless devotion stands between Orsino's sentimental affectation, which covers a deficiency of feeling, and Olivia's excessive grief and equally passionate love. But if Viola expresses in her own love for the Duke the ideal, Feste occupies himself in ridiculing the folly of false love in the others. By catechizing Olivia, the fool points to the absurdity and actual self-indulgence in grieving seven long years for her dead brother. By singing "Come Away, Death," he uncovers the morbid preoccupation in Duke Orsino's pose as the melancholy lover. And by reciting parenthetically the lines of an old ballad, he adds his sly comments on Malvolio's presumption in loving his mistress. As a gentle critic reproving the spurious and sentimental lovers, the fool functions near the center of the play's meaning. There are certain things we feel about Feste which are not explicit in any of the lines in *Twelfth Night*. The essential wholeness or balance in the fool's temperament is one of these. Morris Tilley puts it well when he says that the problem in the play "is the conflict in human nature between the reason and the emotions; and he [Shakespeare] suggests to us in the perfect sanity of Viola and of Feste that the solution lies not in the exclusion of the one or the other, but in the union of the two."[27]

It is no exaggeration of the fool's importance to see him as a moderating influence in the plays—a force on the side of humanity and common sense. This is not to say, as Ulrici does, that in Feste's person "the meaning of the entire poem is as it were concentrated" or that the tragic view of the world "lies hidden in the deep meditative humour of the Fool [in *Lear*] . . ."[28] Nor, on the other hand, can we say that these wise fools are mere excrescences upon the plot. Their roles were not created solely to tickle the pit or to provide acting parts for Robert Armin. The fool in Shakespeare's comic fable and the fool in his tragic fable have several things in common. Both stand a little aside from the main action of their plays, but both serve important dramatic functions. Lear's Fool intensifies the pathos and at the same time humanizes the tragedy for us. In a like manner, Feste tempers the comedy of *Twelfth Night*, simultaneously rendering it gayer and more thoughtful. And in the unusual blending of detachment with sympathy, of irony and pity, the wise fool finds his reason for being.

NOTES

Chapter I. The Fool of Tradition

1. *The Plays of John Marston*, ed. H. Harvey Wood (Edinburgh and London, 1938), II, 150. Wood's edition of Marston's plays has been used throughout.

2. "Le Martyre De S. Pierre Et De S. Paul," ed. M. L. A. Jubinal, in *Mystères inédits du quinzième siècle* (Paris, 1837), I, 78–79.

3. *Illustrations of Shakspeare* (London, 1807), II, 323.

4. *Of the Vanitie and Vncertaintie of Artes and Sciences, Englished by Fa. San gent.* (London, 1569), cap. LXII, sig. Aa3.

5. "A Feast of Lapithae," *The Works of Lucian of Samosata*, tr. H. W. and F. G. Fowler (Oxford, 1905), IV, 134.

6. Allardyce Nicoll, *Masks Mimes and Miracles* (New York, 1931), p. 54. Reich (*Der Mimus*, II, 504) even attempts to trace this bald-headed fool back to a Dorian prototype in the sixth century B.C. performances of the *Deikelistai.*

7. *Geoffrey of Monmouth*, tr. Sebastian Evans ("The Temple Classics," London, 1904), Bk. IX, p. 228.

8. *Twenty Select Colloquies of Erasmus*, tr. Sir Roger L'Estrange (1680), ed. Charles Whibley ("The Abbey Classics," XVII; Boston, n.d.).

9. *The Ship of Fools* (1509), ed. T. H. Jamieson (Edinburgh and London, 1874), I, 181.

10. F. Ficoroni, *Dissertatio de larvis scenicis et figuris comicis antiquorum romanorum* (Rome, 1754), pl. LXXII, 2.

11. *Pulcinella* (Leipzig, 1897), pp. 237–50, 269.

12. *The Passetyme of Pleasure* (1505), ll. 3488–3491, ed. W. E. Mead (Early English Text Society, Original Ser., No. 173; London, 1928).

13. Ll. 191–192, ed. A. Brandl, *Quellen des weltlichen Dramas in England vor Shakespeare* (Strassburg, 1898).

14. *The Medieval Stage* (Oxford, 1903), I, 388.

15. *Dithyramb Tragedy and Comedy* (Oxford, 1927), pp. 245–247.

16. Translated by present author from *Les Comediens en France au moyen âge* (Paris, 1885), p. 147 *n.* Leslie Hotson, *Shakespeare's Motley* (New York, 1952), p. 10, argues that the motley worn by Shakespeare's fools was a coarse, woolen cloth, something like homespun, but "It was *threads*, and *not* segments of material, that were of divers colours; and they were dyed in the wool." However, there are several references to the fool's pied coat in sixteenth century writings from Hawes' *Pastime of Pleasure* (1505) to John Davies of Hereford's *Wit's Pilgrimage* (1605).

17. According to Hotson (pp. 53–54), Shakespeare's fools always wore the long "skirted dress" of the actual idiot. He cites Touchstone's "poke" (*A.Y.L.* II, vii, 20) and Feste's "impeticos" (*Twel.* II, iii, 27) as evidence, but he conveniently forgets the Fool's lines in *Lear* (III, ii, 40): "Marry, here's grace and a codpiece; that's a wise man and a fool." The metaphor would have been meaningless had not the Fool worn that part of the male attire.

18. *Geschichte der Hofnarren* (Liegnitz und Leipzig, 1789), pp. 61–63.

19. *The Honorable Historie of frier Bacon, and frier Bongay*, ll. 157–163, ed. C. M. Gayley, *Representative English Comedies* (New York, 1903), I.

20. *Illustrations of Shakspeare*, II, 319. That the term 'bauble' may have derived etymologically from the Greek βαυβών is suggested by the fact that two characters from Herodas (Mime VI, 19) gossip about a βαυβών, or artificial phallus.

21. Pickard-Cambridge, p. 233.

22. Nicoll, pp. 87–88.

23. Nicoll (p. 269) even tries to trace *Arlecchino*, through his name, back to the bragging Herakles of the mimes and mythological burlesques.

24. Chambers (*Mediaeval Stage*, I, 59–61; II, App. G) cites the hard strictures of Thomas de Cabham, Sub-Dean of Salisbury, in about the year 1213 against several kinds of *histriones*. Cabham recognizes four main groups of entertainers: ballad-singers, makers of romances, satirists, and dancers, tumblers, and mimes.

25. Ibid., I, 68 *n.*

26. Martial (*Epigrams*, Bk. VIII, 13) complains: "Morio dictus erat: viginti milibus emi redde mihi nummos, Gargiliane sapit."

27. Douce, I, 313. Cf. Robert Armin, *A Nest of Ninnies* (1608), ed. J. P. Collier, *Shakespeare Society* (London, 1842), pp. 9, 38.

28. Chambers, in *The Elizabethan Stage* (Oxford, 1923), IV, 260, 269 f, prints extracts from several such acts promulgated during the reigns of Henry VIII and Elizabeth I.

29. Enid Welsford, in *The Fool: His Social and Literary History* (New York, 1935), p. 74, suggests that the fool in exercising his license acts as "a permanent scapegoat whose official duty is to jeer continually at his superiors in order to bear their ill-luck on his own unimportant shoulders." A sort of human lightning rod.

30. Eds. C. L. Brownson and O. J. Todd ("The Loeb Classical Library," London and New York, 1932).

31. II, i, 310, ed. Frederick S. Boas, *The Works of Thomas Kyd* (Oxford, 1901), p. 192.

32. Samuel Rowley, *When You See Me, You Know Me*, ed. K. Elze (Dessau, 1874), pp. 12, 41.

33. John Redford, *Wyt and Science*, ll. 729 f., ed. J. Q. Adams, *Chief Pre-Shakespearean Dramas* (Cambridge, Mass., 1924).

34. Desiderius Erasmus, *The Praise of Folie*, Englished by Sir Thomas Chaloner Knight (London, 1560?), sig. G3.

35. *Misogonus*, I, i, 185, ed. R. W. Bond, *Early Plays from the Italian* (Oxford, 1911). Flögel (*Geschichte der Hofnarren*, p. 74) quotes a variant form of this proverb: "Narren und Kinder reden die Wahrheit."

36. *Common Conditions*, ll. 1731–1775, ed. Tucker Brooke (New Haven, 1915).

37. Athenaeus, *The Deipnosophists*, VI, 248e, tr. C. B. Gulick ("The Loeb Classical Library," London, 1929).

38. *The History of Court Fools* (London, 1858), pp. 6, 9.

39. *The Lives of the Noble Grecians and Romans*, tr. Thomas North (1579), reprinted by Shakespeare Head Press (Stratford-Upon-Avon, 1928), V, 180.

40. Ed. J. Q. Adams, *Chief Pre-Shakespearean Dramas.*

41. Diogenes Laertius, *Lives of Eminent Philosophers*, IX, 59, tr. R. D. Hicks ("The Loeb Classical Library," London, 1925).

42. Ll. 497–504, tr. B. B. Rogers, *Aristophanes* ("The Loeb Classical Library," London, 1924), I.

43. According to the *Tractatus Coislinianus*, ll. 57 f., tr. Lane Cooper, *An Aristotelian Theory of Comedy* (New York, 1922): "The characters (ἤθη) of Comedy are (1) the buffoonish, (2) the ironical, and (3) those of the impostors." In his known extant writings, Aristotle treats of the εἴρων, not as a comical figure, but as the embodiment of a rhetorical figure (*Rhetoric* III, xviii, 1419b) or as a person deficient in the ethical norm of sincerity (*Nic. Eth.* II, vii, [1108a]; IV, vii, [1127a]).

44. Otto Ribbeck, in "Ueber den Begriff des Eiron," *Rheinisches Museum fur Philologie* (Frankfurt am Main, 1876), XXXI, 382, characterizes this early ironical man as no pleasant person: "Der Fuchs ist also unter den Thieren der eigentliche Typus dieses Charakters, der unter der Maske der Harmlosigkeit mit glatten Vorwänden betrügende Schalk und sein grades Gegentheil der Ehrliche (ἁπλοῦς, ὄρθιος). Es war also gewiss kein Compliment, wenn dem Sokrates von seinen

Zeitgenossen und Gegnern εἰρωνεία und εἰρωνεύεσθαι zugeschrieben wurde, sondern ein Ausdruck des Unwillens und der Erbitterung uber seine Art, die Leute gesprächsweise zu foppen."

45. J. A. K. Thomson, in *Irony: An Historical Introduction* (London, 1926), p. 181, points to Plato's complete reversal of Socrates' role in Aristophanes' comedy: "In the *Clouds* Socrates is the *Alazon* or Villain of the piece, in the *Dialogues* he is the *Eiron* or Hero." However, Aristophanes is not always as careful to differentiate the ironical man from the boastful impostor as is Aristotle or Dr. Thomson. The buffoon Strepsiades (*The Clouds*, l. 449) describes himself by turns as εἴρων and as ἀλαζών.

46. *Symposium*, 215–16, tr. B. Jowett, *The Dialogues of Plato* (New York, 1937).

47. Brandt and Barclay include among their ships' passengers not only personifications of medieval vices and vanities but also the traditional impostors—pedantical clerks, foppish gallants, and boastful babblers—such as have often walked the boards of the comic stage.

48. Plate I for *Moriae Encomium, id est: Stultitiae Laus*, in Desiderii Erasmi Roterodami *Opera Omnia* (Leyden, 1703), IV, 406.

Chapter II. EMERGENCE OF THE STAGE FOOL

1. J. Mortensen, in *Le Théâtre français au moyen âge* (Paris, 1903), p. 203, states that: "La sotie, comme son nom nous indique, était un genre réservé aux «sots» ou fous; et de même que la fête des fous parodiait la hiérarchie, de même la sotie ridiculisait la société du moyen âge en général."

2. *Farce Moralle et joyeuse des Sobres Sotz*, ll. 128–30, ed. Émile Picot, in *Recueil Général des Sotties, III* (Paris, 1912), 61.

3. Ibid., ll. 316–22.

4. *Studies in the Literary Relations of England and Germany in the Sixteenth Century* (Cambridge, 1886), p. 271 *n*.

5. *Bibliothek des litterarischen Vereins*, XXIX (Stuttgart, 1853), 526.

6. Ibid.

7. *All For Money*, ll. 529–34, ed. E. Vogel, in *Shakespeare Jahrbuch*, XL (Berlin, 1904). Moros, the Vice-fool in Wager's *The longer thou liuest, the more foole thou art* (c. 1559), ll. 1842 f., exclaims: "If it please the Deuill me to haue, / Let him carry me away on his back." And the poor scholar Miles, in Greene's *Friar Bacon and Friar Bungay*, rides to Hell on the Devil's back at the close of the play.

8. *The Devil and the Vice in the English Dramatic Literature before Shakespeare* (Halle, 1900), p. 145. R. L. Ramsay, in the excellent introduction to his edition of Skelton's *Magnyfycence* (Early English Text Society, Ext. Ser., No. 98; London, 1908), p. xc, criticizes Cushman for basing his argument on Vice figures in the degenerate moral plays written and produced after 1550.

9. Ed. J. Q. Adams, in *Chief Pre-Shakespearean Dramas*, p. 337.

10. Ed. A. Brandl, in *Shakespeare Jahrbuch*, XXXVI (Berlin, 1900).

11. Ed. Herbert Davis (The Malone Society Reprints; Oxford, 1952).

12. Ed. J. S. Farmer (The Tudor Facsimile Texts; London, 1908), sig. D3.

13. Preface, *Joseph Andrews*, ed. Leslie Stephen, in *The Works of Henry Fielding, Esq*. (London, 1882), IV, xv. Cf. Thomas Wilson, *The Arte of Rhetorique*, ed. G. H. Mair ("Tudor & Stuart Library"; Oxford, 1909), p. 137: "and as for wretched soules or poore bodies, none can beare to haue them mocked, but thinke rather that thei should be pitied, except they foolishly vaunt them selues."

14. Ed. W. W. Greg, in *Materialien zur Kunde des älteren englischen Dramas*, V (Louvain, 1904).

15. Ibid., pp. x, xi.

16. Ed. J. Q. Adams, in *Chief Pre-Shakespearean Dramas*, p. 305.

17. John Metham uses this expression to describe the style of Lydgate in the Epilogue to Metham's romance of *Amoryus and Cleopes* (1448/9), ed. Hardin Craig (Early English Text Society, Orig. Ser., No. 132; London, 1916), p. 80.

18. *Lusty Juventus*, sig. D1, ed. J. S. Farmer ("Old English Drama, Students' Facsimile Edition"; Amersham, England, n.d.).

19. Ed. Tucker Brooke (New Haven, Conn., 1915).

20. Ll. 4502–12, ed. Douglas Hamer, in *The Works of Sir David Lindsay* (Edinburgh and London, 1931), II. *Mère-Sotte* of Gringore's *Sottie contre le pape Jules II* (1512), ed. Picot, II, tries to seduce prelates and ween nobles away from the Prince of Sots by offering them "chapeaux rouges." The parallel is not precise, but the stage business of distributing hats is essentially the same.

21. *A Booke of Precedence*, ed. F. J. Furnivall (Early English Text Society, Ext. Ser., No. 8; London, 1869), pp. 77–78.

22. Ed. and tr. L. R. Merrill, *The Life and Poems of Nicholas Grimald* ("Yale Studies in English," LXIX; New Haven, Conn., 1925).

23. Petit de Julleville, in *Le Théâtre en France* (Paris, 1908), p. 66, gives the following definition: "Le sermon joyeux est né de la fête des Fous; le premier qui s'avisa, dans l'ivresse bruyante de la fête, de monter dans la chaire chretienne et parodier le predicateur dans une improvisation bachique, debita la premier sermon joyeux."

24. Ed. and tr. E. R. Payne (New Haven, Conn., 1938).

25. Ed. A. E. H. Swaen (The Malone Society Reprints; Oxford, 1921).

26. Doran, *History of Court Fools*, p. 152.

Chapter III. Elizabethan Fools and Clowns

1. Intermeane after Act I, eds. C. H. Herford and P. Simpson, in *Ben Jonson* (Oxford, 1938), VI, 302. Herford and Simpson's edition of Jonson's plays has been used throughout.

2. Authority for this statement comes directly from the Induction to the play. To Sly's query, "What are your additions?" Burbadge answers: "Sooth not greatly needefull, only as your sallet to your greate feast, to entertaine a little more time, and to abridge the not received custome of musicke in our Theater" (ll. 82–85, ed. Wood, I, 143).

3. If H. R. Walley, in "The Dates of *Hamlet* and Marston's *The Malcontent*," *R.E.S.*, IX (October, 1933), pp. 397–409, is right in asserting that *The Malcontent* was not written before 1604, then Passarello could be a pale reflection of Shakespeare's Lavache, whom he resembles more closely than he does Feste.

4. Kathleen M. Lea, *Italian Popular Comedy* (Oxford, 1934), I, 68.

5. Cf. Satyre III, *The Scourge of Villanie*, ed. G. B. Harrison ("Bodley Head Quartos," No. 13; London, 1925), pp. 28 f.

6. Ed. A. H. Bullen, *The Works of Thomas Middleton* (London, 1885), IV, 319.

7. "A Pleasant Tale of Will Sommers," *The Defence of Conny Catching* (1592), ed. A. B. Grosart, *The Life and Complete Works of Robert Greene* ("The Huth Library," London, 1881–1886), XI, 71.

8. *A Nest of Ninnies*, pp. 46–47.

9. Armin (pp. 41 f.) gives Will a generous disposition: "He was a poor man's friend, / And help'd the widow often in her end. / The King would ever grant what he did crave, / For well he knew Will no exacting knave; / But wish'd the King to do good deeds great store, / Which caused the court to love him more and more."

10. *A Mirrovr of Monsters* (London, 1587), fol. 7, sig. C3. The Folger Shakespeare Library copy.

11. Ed. J. B. Leishman, *The Three Parnassus Plays* (1598–1601) (London, 1949).

12. George Wilkins, *The Miseries of Inforst Mariage*, ed. J. S. Farmer ("Old English Drama, Students' Facsimile Edition," 1913), sig. A2.

13. *A Biographical Chronicle of the English Drama, 1559–1642* (London, 1891), II, 276. Chambers (*Eliz. Stage.* III, 513) suggests that Robin's jigging rhyme refers to Kempe's famous morris dance from London to Norwich.

14. Ed. Fredson Bowers, in *The Dramatic Works of Thomas Dekker* (Cambridge, 1953), I, 179. Bowers' edition used throughout.

15. I, ii, 311, ed. F. Bowers, I, 225.

16. Ll. 435–37, ed. Kenneth W. Cameron (Raleigh, N. C., 1941).

Chapter IV. Shakespeare's Wise Fools

1. *Falstaff and Other Shakespearean Topics* (New York, 1925), p. 75.

2. *As You Like It*, New Variorum ed. (Philadelphia, 1890), p. 309.

3. T. W. Baldwin, in "Shakespeare's Jester," *MLN*, XXXIX (1924), 447–55, presents convincing evidence for dating Armin's joining the Chamberlain's Men in 1600, after publication of his *Quips Upon Questions.* Chambers, in *Eliz. Stage,* II, 300, accepts the *Quips* as Armin's but somewhat inconsistently dates Armin's entry into Shakespeare's company 1599, because he describes himself on the title page of the first edition of *Quips* as "Clonnico de Curtanio Snuffe."

4. This diminishing or debasing of a thing or a person is known to rhetoricians as meiosis, or the disabler (Puttenham, Bk. III, Ch. xvii). Rosemond Tuve, in *Elizabethan and Metaphysical Imagery* (Chicago, 1947), p. 206, notes the "tempering or astringent effect" of such a figure and its ironical implications.

5. "Ueber Shakespeare's Narren," *Shakespeare Jahrbuch*, IX (Weimar, 1874), p. 104 f.

6. Whether Touchstone's parody on the courtly manner of quarreling specifically lampoons Vincentio Saviolo's *Honor and honorable Quarrels* (1595) or another work, *The Book of Honor and Arms* (1590) does not greatly matter. Through the fool, Shakespeare takes a dig at all such popular handbooks.

7. Cf. Feliche, in *Antonio and Mellida* (III, i, 226), on the fantastic, perfumed gull Castilio: "Honest musk-cod, twill not be so stitched together; take that, and that [striking him], and belie no Ladies love: sweare no more by Jesu: this Madam, that Ladie; hence goe, forsweare the presence, travaile three years to bury this bastinado: avoide, puffe paste, avoide."

8. *The Allegory of Love* (Oxford, 1948), pp. 172, 173.

9. For a contrary opinion, see F. S. Boas, *Shakspere and his Predecessors* (New York, 1896), pp. 339 f.: "Touchstone's wit takes always and with every one a caustic turn. . . . Thus while, like Feste, he has to do with each of the characters in turn, he notes their special disposition, not to chime in with it, or to gently hint a cure for its defects, but to throw it up in all its worst lights." Such a description would fit Jaques more easily than Touchstone.

10. *Comic Characters of Shakespeare* (London, 1946), p. 36.

11. *Shakespeare* (New York, 1939), p. 169.

12. *Shakespeare Commentaries,* tr. F. E. Bunnett (London, 1880), p. 438.

13. *Nichomachean Ethics* ii, 7, tr. J. E. C. Welldon (London and New York, 1892).

14. *Epistulae ad Familiares* IX, xxii, 4, tr. W. Glynn Williams ("The Loeb Classical Library"; Cambridge, Mass. and London, 1952).

15. We must not pass on without noting one further use Shakespeare makes of this aphorism. In *Lear* IV, i, 46, Gloucester returns more nearly to the letter and spirit of the original: "'Tis the time's plague when madmen lead the blind."

16. John W. Draper, in *The Twelfth Night of Shakespeare's Audience* (Stanford, Cal., 1950), p. 208, regards Feste as a shrewd *arriviste* and little better than Malvolio as an impostor and time-server. Such a reading of Feste's character misses completely the charm and the gay impudence of the fool.

17. *Shakespeare: A Survey* (New York, 1926), p. 177.

18. *Shakespeare's Bawdy* (London, 1947), p. 53.

19. Cf. Middleton, *A Chaste Maid in Cheapside* I, ii, 17, ed. Bullen, *Works*, V, 17.

20. W. W. Lawrence, "The Meaning of *All's Well*," *PMLA*, XXXVII (1922), 459.

21. In his speech, Lavache comes the closest of Shakespeare's fools to being a scurrilous buffoon. There is still a vast difference between his sometimes unsavory similes and the snarling scurrilities of a Thersites or a Buffone.

22. "Fool in Lear," *The Sewanee Review*, LVII (April-June, 1949), 183. For another study of *Lear* which makes much of the Fool's role, see Robert Heilman, *This Great Stage: Image and Structure in King Lear* (Baton Rouge, La., 1948).

23. *Coleridge's Shakespearean Criticism*, ed. T. M. Raysor (Cambridge, Mass., 1930), I, 63.

24. *Shakspere and his Predecessors*, p. 444.

25. *N.E.D.* V, 622: "applied as a common noun to a homely woman, maid-servant, sweetheart or mistress; or as a term of disparagement." Cf. *Cambises*, 252: "Meretrix. Gog hart, slave, doost thinke I am a sixpeny iug?" and *Knack to Know a Knave*, 178: "Then comes a soldier counterfeit, and with him his jug."

26. *King Lear*, New Variorum ed. (Philadelphia, 1880), p. 174*n.* Shakespeare uses a somewhat analogous figure in Menenius Agrippa's fable of the mutiny against the belly (*Cor.* I, i, 99).

27. This fool obviously wears an exaggerated form of that appendage to male attire of doublet and hose, not the long, yellow gown of the village idiot in which Hotson insists on dressing him.

28. To an almost identical comment, the Fool in *Timon* answers even more pointedly:

VAR. SERV. Thou art not altogether a fool.

FOOL. Nor thou altogether a wise man. As much foolery as I have, so much wit thou lack'st. (II, ii, 122)

This brothel fool is somewhat akin to Lavache in his wit and his bawdry, but his appearance is altogether too brief to warrant treating him as one of Shakespeare's wise fools. Besides, these lines are not ascribed to Shakespeare by Fleay or by E. H. Wright, *The Authorship of Timon of Athens* (New York, 1910).

29. *Shakespearean Tragedy* (1904, 2 ed. New York, 1949), p. 312.

30. Ibid., pp. 312–13.

31. *The Living Shakespeare* (New York, 1949), p. 876.

32. *Shakespearean Tragedy*, p. 308.

33. *The Plays of William Shakespeare* (London, 1773), IX, 382 *n.*

34. *Prefaces to Shakespeare, First Series* (London, 1927), p. 200.

Chapter V. Critic in Motley

1. Welsford, *The Fool*, p. 224.

2. *Euery Man out of his Humour*, eds. C. H. Herford and Percy Simpson, in *Ben Jonson* (Oxford, 1927), III, 450–51. Herford and Simpson's edition of Jonson's plays has been used throughout.

3. M. H. Shackford (Ed.), *As You Like It* ("The Tudor Shakespeare"; New York, 1926), p. xv.

4. "Shakspere, Marston, and the Malcontent Type," *MP*, III (June 1905), 282, 287. Using his own chronology for the plays of Marston, Stoll traces the "Malcontent Type" back from Jaques and Hamlet to Marston's Malevole and Feliche to the pre-Shakespearean Hamlet, bringing his line of descent almost full circle.

5. "Jaques and the Malcontent Traveler," *PQ*, XIV (July 1935), 237 ff.

6. "Jaques," *The Huntington Library Bulletin*, No. 8 (Oct. 1935), p. 84.

7. Some commentators have mistaken the jaundiced views of the malcontent Jaques for Shakespeare's mature reflections on life. More astute critics remember

that Shakespeare seldom speaks through the characters in his plays but that he sometimes lends to rogues and scoundrels a certain spurious dignity by breathing fine poetry into their speeches.

8. Jonson probably got some of the details for his description of Carlo as a backbiter from Horace's defence of his own satire:

absentem qui rodit amicum,
qui non defendit alio culpante, solutos
qui captat risus hominum famaque dicacis,
fingere qui non visa potest, commissa tacere
qui nequit: hic niger est, hunc tu, Romane, caveto.
(Satires I, iv, 81–85)

In this passage, Horace distinguishes between the merely abusive detractor and the impersonal satirist. However, in the very next *Satire* (I, v, 70), Horace apparently delights in a battle of defamation between two railing buffoons.

9. "Shakespeare's *Troilus and Cressida* Yet Deeper in Its Tradition," in *Essays in Dramatic Literature: The Parrott Presentation Volume*, ed. Hardin Craig (Princeton, 1935), p. 154.

10. *Comicall Satyre and Shakespeare's Troilus and Cressida* (San Marino, Cal., 1938), p. 203.

11. *The Iliad of Homer. Translated according to the Greek by George Chapman*, ed. I. Gollancz ("The Temple Classics"; London, 1898), Bk. II, ll. 181–85.

12. *Nicomachean Ethics* IV, xiv, tr. J. E. C. Welldon (London, 1892).

13. *The Characters of Theophrastus*, tr. J. M. Edmonds ("The Loeb Classical Library"; London, 1942).

14. *De Oratore* II, lxi, 251, tr. E. W. Sutton and H. Rackham ("The Loeb Classical Library"; London, 1929), p. 385.

15. Ed. G. H. Mair ("Tudor & Stuart Library"; Oxford, 1909).

16. *Wits Miserie and the Worlds Madness* (1596), in *Complete Works of Thomas Lodge* (The Hunterian Club; Glasgow, 1883), II, 84.

17. *Philebus* 50, in *The Dialogues of Plato*, tr. B. Jowett (Oxford, 1871): "when we laugh at the folly of our friends, pleasure, in mingling with envy, mingles with pain, for envy has been acknowledged by us to be mental pain, and laughter is pleasant; and so we envy and laugh at the same instant." Jowett's translation of Plato's *Dialogues* has been used throughout.

18. *The Ancren Riwle. A Treatise on the Rules and Duties of Monastic Life*, ed. and tr. James Morton (The Camden Society; London, 1853), LVII, 211, 213.

19. Although Jonson in *E.M.O.* gives us a gallery of gulls and two railing satirists to exhibit them, he gives us no witty fool or genial humorist. The reason is not hard to find. For all his learning in the classics, Jonson's comic muse is a rather humorless creature. She is not compact of irony and pity, as is the muse of Shakespeare. Baskervill, *English Elements in Jonson's Early Comedy* (Austin, Texas, 1911), p. 32, explains that "the serious message, the uncompromising bluntness that belong to him as a middleclass Englishman spoil any lightness and play, any subtle mockery and laughing irony that we might expect from a genuine literary attitude to the objects of satire. Invective and arraignment are dominant in Jonson's work as in the age."

20. Rowley, *When You See Me*, pp. 77–78.

21. Although Will Summers (Rowley p. 41) censures King Henry VIII, he upbraids him not for his tyranny but for his too great lenity toward Wolsey. And Lear's Fool continually berates his King for his unwise liberality in dividing up his realm. Shakespeare usually assigns satire on corrupt and abusive kingly authority to spokesmen such as the buffoon Thersites (*Troi.* II, iii, 9; V, i, 56; V, iv, 1) and the malcontent Prince Hamlet (I, v, 106).

22. *Materialien*, V (1904), pp. x, xi.

23. *A pleasant History of the Life and Death of Will Summers* (London, 1637), sigs. C6, C7. Folger Shakespeare Library copy. I wish here to express my thanks to the authorities of the Folger Library for permission to see this and other rare books which I have consulted for this study.

24. The Biblical inspiration for this little rhyme is obvious:

A whip for the horse, a bridle for the ass,
And a rod for the back of fools. (Prov. xxvi, 3)

25. *The Birds*, ll. 903–1469, tr. B. B. Rogers ("The Loeb Classical Library"; London and New York, 1924).

26. Cf. O. J. Campbell, "*Love's Labour's Lost* Re-studied," *Studies in Shakespeare, Milton and Donne* ("University of Michigan Publications, Language and Literature," I; New York, 1925), pp. 24, 26 *n*. See also Lea, *Italian Popular Comedy*, I, 50–52.

27. The alchemist as a wily impostor creeps into much medieval and renaissance literature, from Chaucer's *Canon's Yeoman's Tale* to Erasmus' *Colloquy* XV. An early instance of the quack alchemist on the stage is that of Falset in Lindsay's *Ane Satyre*. He reveals his knavery in the following lines:

And I haue greit intelligence
In quelling of the quintessence:
Bot to preif my experience,
Sir len me fourtie crownes (ll. 886–9)

28. Cf. P. Mueschke and J. Fleisher, "Jonsonian Elements in the Comic Underplot of Twelfth Night," *PMLA*, XLVIII (1933), p. 724: "These types of social affectation, characteristic of the would-be (who would be be witty or cultured or fashionable or anything other than he is) are conditioned by Jonson's conception of the Renaissance gentleman—ideally a combination of the best qualities in a soldier and a man of letters with the social graces of a courtier."

29. *The Complete Poems*, ed. A. B. Grosart (London, 1876), II, 9.

30. O. J. Campbell (*Comicall Satyre*, p. 21) explains the threat that the *nouveau riche* citizen represented: "the persistence and intensity of the attack made upon the upstarts demand a more adequate explanation than their offensive manners. This may be found in the threat which such parvenus, amply provided with plenty of easy money, made to the traditional cohesions and groupings of English society. The old aristocracy, and the writers catering to it, followed a sound instinct of self-preservation in repelling with all their intellectual and moral energy the imminent disruption of their social world."

31. Conservatives in Shakespeare's audience might well have seen in Malvolio a symbol of the rising moneyed classes, which threatened to overturn not only the cakes and ale but also the unstable props of the Elizabethan compromise.

32. Among the several attempts to identify Malvolio with some contemporary of Shakespeare's, that of I. Gollancz, in *A Book of Homage to Shakespeare* (Oxford, 1916), pp. 177 f., is most interesting. His candidate is Sir Ambrose Willoughby, Queen Elizabeth's Chief Sewer and Squire of the Presence. And although "it would have been a congenial task to hit [him] off on the stage," Sir Ambrose is disqualified by the color of his blood. Malvolio, as Draper, in "Olivia's Household," *PMLA*, LXIX (1934), 797–806, explains, is no gentleman but an upstart servant whose presumption is punished.

33. "Parolles," in *Shaksperian Studies*, eds. B. Matthews and A. Thorndike (New York, 1916), p. 295.

34. Could Lavache have been reading Quintilian's injunction (VIII, vi, 14) against sordid and gross metaphors?

35. Baskervill (p. 186) traces the pretentious gull and the upstart courtier from the allegorical figure of Pride in the moralities, down through the satirical pamphlets of Greene and Nashe to the verse satire of Hall, Marston, Guilpin, and Davies, to where he reappears on the stage in the humour comedies of Chapman and Jonson.

36. In the Induction to *E.M.O.*, Asper threatens to scourge all such apes of fashion who "in wearing a pyed feather, / The cable hat-band, or the three-pild ruffe, / A yard of shooetye, or the *Switzers* knot / On his *French* garters, should affect a Humour!" (ll. 110–13).

37. Orange in Jonson's *E.M.O.* strolls about, uttering "O Lord sir" and "O God sir" continually.

38. O. J. Campbell (*The Living Shakespeare*, p. 622 *n*) suggests a covert rebuke of Sir Andrew's parsimony in this seeming nonsense.

39. *The Praise of Folly* 9, tr. Hoyt H. Hudson (Princeton, N. J., 1941), p. 26.

40. Ll. 192–96, tr. E. H. Sugden, in *The Complete Roman Drama*, ed. G. E. Duckworth (New York, 1942), I, 170.

41. Lea, I, 167. Cf. W. Smith, *The Commedia Dell 'Arte* (New York, 1912), p. 14 *n*. Miss Smith quotes a zanni from *Gl'amorosi inganni* (I, xiii) in the following unromantic view of love: "This love has made you timid, from a brave man it has turned you into a coward, from a wise man into a fool, from sensible to silly, from a Spanish charger it has changed you into a mule, for from the hour you fell in love you have made nothing but trouble, singing your sonnet nonsense through the streets, your Petrarch in your fist."

42. Lea, I, 204. Cf. Scenario *Li Ritratti* II, tr. Lea, II, 565.

43. Lea, II, 405, 431–53. Cf. W. Smith, "Italian and Elizabethan Comedy," *MP*, V (1908), 7–8; O. J. Campbell, "*Love's Labour's Lost* Re-studied," pp. 26–28, and "*The Two Gentlemen of Verona* and Italian Comedy," pp. 49–63, both in *Studies in Shakespeare, Milton and Donne*. A letter dated 13 Jan. 1578 from the Privy Council to the Lord Mayor requiring a permit for "one Drousiano, an Italian, a commediante and his companye" to play in London until the first week in Lent and an item in the Chamber Accounts for April 1577 are the only clear evidences that a *Commedia* troupe ever played in England. The external evidence that Shakespeare ever saw a performance of the *Commedia* is slight, but there is abundant proof from his plays that he knew such stock figures as pantalone, capitano, and zanni.

44. Miss Lea (I, 186) distinguishes between the two: "A 'burla' . . . is something between a 'lazzo,' or comic turn, and a regular subplot, and should involve an action which ties a knot that must be cut or undone before the play can proceed."

45. Ducharte, in *The Italian Comedy*, tr. R. T. Weaver (London, 1929), p. 146, gives us an excerpted dialogue from an unidentified play in which the traditionally stupid Harlequin shows something of Touchstone's wit:

> HARLEQUIN. Once more, mademoiselle, allow me to tell you that I am not the first rascal that love has made tolerable. I present you my heart larded with your graces, trussed up with your charms, and steeped in your attractions. Come, mademoiselle, it will mean nothing to you and everything to me if you will exchange an amorous glance with a poor devil greedy of your youth and beauty. Gaze upon me and observe how my passion shows despite the livery I wear.
>
> ISABELLE. You are making fun at my expense, sir!
>
> HARLEQUIN. Alas, if you but knew how deeply I am smitten. If you'd consent, so help me, I should be foolish enough to marry you.

46. At the risk of appearing to elaborate the obvious, we should note that, highly compressed though it is, Touchstone's speech shows all the characteristics of the burlesque panegyric. It belongs to the same genre as Erasmus' *Moriae Encomium* and Swift's *A Digression Concerning Madness*. The speech uses what Worcester, in *The Art of Satire* (Cambridge, Mass., 1940), p. 80, calls the irony of inversion, a device by which the reader is made to convert apparent praise into blame.

47. Rowley, *When You See Me*, pp. 48, 49.

48. Touchstone's affectation of learning used to overawe Corin and William (V, i, 44) serves also a parody on the schoolbook logic and rhetoric of his time. By his playful use of enthymeme (I, ii, 81), full syllogism (III, iii, 91), comic sorites (III, ii, 41), and chop logic, the fool shows his familiarity with such con-

temporary works as Wilson's *The Rule of Reason* (1551) or Blundeville's *The Art of Logicke* (1599).

49. *A Discourse Concerning the Original and Progress of Satire*, ed. W. P. Ker, in *Essays of John Dryden* (Oxford, 1900), II, 92–93.

50. *Comic Characters of Shakespeare*, p. 46.

51. "Shakspere, Marston, and the Malcontent Type," p. 282.

52. *An Humorous Day's Mirth*, ed. D. Nichol Smith ("The Malone Society Reprints"; Oxford, 1938), ll. 925–40.

53. Marston, *The Scourge of Villanie*, ed. G. B. Harrison ("Bodley Head Quartos," No. XIII; London, 1925), pp. 125–26.

54. *How Shakespeare 'Purged' Jonson: A Problem Solved* (Cambridge, 1928), p. 5. Gray gives his own case away when, at the end of the essay (p. 34), he abandons his earlier position and says that "Jaques stands, not for Jonson, but for Jonsonian 'Humour'."

55. Satyre II, ll. 157–60, ed. A. B. Grosart, in *The Poems of John Marston* (Manchester, 1879).

56. "Jaques," *Huntington Library Bulletin*, No. 8, pp. 100, 102.

57. Cf. Pickard-Cambridge, in *Dithyramb Tragedy and Comedy*, p. 270: "A considerable part of many plays of Aristophanes consists of scenes in which a person of absurd or extravagant pretensions is derided or made a fool of by a person who plays the buffoon—scenes (to use the convenient Greek terms) between an ἀλαζών and βωμολόχος." See also F. Cornford, in *The Origin of Attic Comedy* (London, 1914), p. 156: "Dikaiopolis plays Buffoon, and uses his 'irony' to discountenance this bragging Impostor, and beat him from the field of argument."

Chapter VI. The Fool in the Fable

1. E. E. Stoll, in *John Webster* (Cambridge, Mass., 1905), p. 60, attempts to backdate these additions to 1600 from an allusion to a horn "growing in the womans forehead twelve yeeres since" in a speech of Passarello's (I, vii, 108). H. R. Walley, in "The Dates of *Hamlet* and Marston's *The Malcontent*," pp. 403–4, disagrees about the dating, preferring 1604. He is convinced also that Passarello, who appears nowhere in the play but in this set of insertions, was added to the earlier Paul's play when it was adapted for the popular stage and presented by the King's Men.

2. Henry VIII speaks the greatest number of lines (1051), but Will comes next with 374 lines as against 246 lines for Wolsey and 152 lines for Queen Katherine. Will speaks more lines than does any of Shakespeare's fools. Feste comes closest with 357 lines, Touchstone next with 321 lines, Lear's Fool has 263 lines, and Lavache but 221. Feste, however, speaks more lines relative to the length of the play than does Summers, and Lear's Fool speaks proportionately more during the time that he is in the play.

As for the length of time the fool spends on the stage, Feste again leads with nine entrances, appearing in about half the scenes of the play. Will Summers is on stage about forty percent of the time; whereas Touchstone and Lavache appear about one third of the time in their plays. Lear's Fool, though he is in only about one fourth of the play, has a relatively full part during that time. The parts of Passarello, Pickadill, and Dondolo together (415 ll.) aggregate little more than Summers' role in length. Although such objective criteria are no absolute measure of the importance of the fool to his play, they are indicative of the playwright's intent.

3. Dedicatory Epistle to *The Right Excellent and famous Historye, of Promos and Cassandra* ("Old English Drama, Students' Facsimile Edition"). (Amersham, Eng., 1913?), sig. A2v.

4. *An Apologie for Poetrie* (c. 1583, printed 1595), ed. G. G. Smith, in *Elizabethan Critical Essays* (Oxford, 1904), I, 199.

NOTES

5. Cicero, in *De Optimo Genere Oratorum* I, i, tr. H. M. Hubbell ("The Loeb Classical Library"; London, 1949), decrees: "Itaque et in tragoedia comicum vitiosum est et in comoedia turpe tragicum." And Horace, in *Ars Poetica,* ll. 231–33, observes:

effutire levis indigna Tragoedia versus,
ut festis matrona moveri iussa diebus,
intererit Satyris paulum pudibunda protervis.

Horace, of course, speaks of the Satyr play, an afterpiece to the tragic trilogy, not to be confused with the purely comic play.

6. *The Arte of English Poesie,* Bk. III, Ch. xxiv, ed. G. D. Willcock and A. Walker (Cambridge, 1936), p. 277. At another place (p. 263), Puttenham defines decorum not as a static quality but as a variable relationship depending upon circumstances.

7. Horace (*Ars Poetica,* 119) advises the poet: "Aut famam sequere aut sibi convenientia finge." Cicero (*Orator* xxii, 74) expresses the same thought: "quod si poeta fugit ut maximum vitium qui peccat etiam, cum probam orationem affingit improbo stultove sapientis." But Cicero elsewhere (*De Oratore* II, lxviii, 274) recognizes that there are times when a wise man may speak in the manner of a fool.

8. Ed. J. Q. Adams, in *Chief Pre-Shakespearean Dramas.*

9. Horace (*Ars Poetica,* 105) cautions:

tristia maestum
voltum verba decent, iratum plena minarum,
ludentem lasciva, severum seria dictu.

10. F. M. Padelford, *Select Translations from Scaliger's Poetics,* Bk. I, Ch. vi ("Yale Studies in English," XXVI; New York, 1905), p. 39.

11. Ibid., Bk. IV, Ch. ii. Horace (*Ars Poetica,* 92–98) suggests a need for flexibility in fitting style to dramatic subject:

singula quaeque locum teneant sortita decentem.
interdum tamen et vocem Comoedia tollit,
iratusque Chremes tumido delitigat ore;
et tragicus plerumque dolet sermone pedestri
Telephus et Peleus, cum pauper et exsul uterque
proicit ampullas et sesquipedalia verba,
si curat cor spectantis tetigisse querella.

12. The deliberate debasing a person or a thing to its clean contrary goes beyond simple metaphor or meiosis. Puttenham (Bk. III, Ch. xvii) would probably have labelled this dark image *Catachresis* or the Figure of Abuse. See also Tuve, *Elizabethan and Metaphysical Imagery,* pp. 130–33.

13. Cicero (*Orator* xxiii, 81) believes that metaphor is appropriate to a plain style because it is used often in the speech of rustics.

14. "Robert Armine, The Foole," *PMLA,* xlii (1927), p. 684.

15. *King Lear,* ed. D. N. Smith, The [American] Arden Shakespeare (Boston, 1917), p. xvii. Smith surely does not mean that the Fool acts only as a comic relief in an otherwise bleak tragedy. Gelasimus, through his cynical comments, serves as a comic foil to the tragedy of John and the romantic love of Herod and Herodias in Grimald's *Archipropheta,* but his role is very different from that of the Fool in *Lear.*

16. *De Oratore* II, lxvii, 269 ff.: "Urbana etiam dissimulatio est, cum alia dicuntur ac sentias, non illo genere de quo ante dixi, cum contraria dicas . . . sed cum toto genere orationis severe ludas, cum aliter sentias ac loquare."

17. Dr. Thümmel gives us an interesting and provocative study in his "Über Shakespeare's Narren." However, when he attempts to place Shakespeare's four principal fools in the Procrustean bed of his analysis (pp. 96–97), he has to chop them down to size and mangle their features. Certainly Feste is good-humored in his fooling, but he is also artful and sophisticated, not naive.

18. L. Cazamian, in *L'Humour de Shakespeare* (Paris, 1945), p. 138, expresses the tone of Feste's irony: "son ironie n'est pas sans bonté, et sa tristesse n'est jamais amère." According to E. J. West, in "Bradleyan Reprise: On the Fool in *Twelfth Night*," *Shakespeare Assn. Bull.*, XXIV (Oct. 1949), p. 266: "Feste is frequently ironic; but I submit that his irony is that of his own realization of his intellectual superiority and not that of James Thurber's indubitably and profoundly revealing contemporary Middle Aged man."

19. Friedrich Schlegel and Ludwig Tieck were the two parents of *die romantische Ironie*. If Schlegel fathered the idea, Tieck brought it forth in all its monstrous proportions. Their creature has usurped the place of the Greek thing and has all but smothered genuine irony under a veil of cosmic mysticism. Elizabethans, of course, were unfamiliar with any such monstrous conception. People in Shakespeare's audience were familiar with rhetorical irony in its several forms: the "Merry Scoffe," the "Bitter Tawnt," and the "Drie Mock" (Puttenham, Bk. III, Ch. xviii). They would have regarded certain individuals as consistently ironical in their behavior, but they would have called such persons "pleasant."

20. Kittredge, in *Shakspere: An Address* (Cambridge, Mass., 1916), p. 40, emphatically protests against taking Shakespeare's characters "as embodiments of this or that ethical concept." No reasonable person would question the soundness of Professor Kittredge's advice. However, we ought also to remember that a playwright must use the only material he has at hand—his characters—to give life to the ideas or emotions in his play.

21. T. W. Baldwin (*William Shakspere's Small Latine and lesse Greeke* [Urbana, Ill., 1944], II, 667) remarks: "If Shakspere ever heard of Aristotle, it was the Aristotle of his own age, not that of Greece, still less that of the latest expert."

22. Ibid., II, 591 ff. Cf. Heinsius, *Ad Horatii de Plauto et Terentio judicium dissertatio*, in *Terentii Comoediae Sex* (1651), p. **2ᵛ.

23. *Comic Theory in the Sixteenth Century* (Urbana, Ill., 1950), p. 131. Herrick credits Petrus Marsus, a fifteenth century Terentian commentator, with seeing this Aristotelian scheme in the Terence play. But Marsus, in his comments on *Adelphi* V, ix, 958, in *P. Terentii Afri Lepidissimi Comoediae* (Paris, 1552), p. 508, merely cites the *Nicomachean Ethics* to point out the dishonesty in prodigality.

24. *The Arte of Rhetorique*, p. 139. Cf. Castiglione, *The Book of The Courtier . . . Done into English by Sir Thomas Hoby (1561)*, ed. Walter Raleigh (London, 1900), p. 153: "thei [common jesters] have no respecte to the condicion of the person they commune withall, to the place where they be, to the time, to the gravitie and modestye which they ought to have in themselves."

25. Professor Cazamian (p. 141) goes too far in his admiration of Feste's perspicacity: "il devine au premier moment que Cesario est une femme, et qu'il s'agit d'une aventure de coeur." Anyone acquainted with Elizabethan dramatic conventions must know that the flimsiest disguise was never penetrable by other characters.

26. *The Play: A Critical Anthology* (New York, 1951), p. 368.

27. "Organic Unity of Twelfth Night," *PMLA*, xxix (1914), pp. 556–57.

28. *Shakspeare's Dramatic Art*, tr. A. J. W. M. (London, 1846), pp. 198, 250.

INDEX

INDEX

INDEX

INDEX

INDEX

INDEX